QUEST FOR TRUTH

SCIENTIFIC PROGRESS AND RELIGIOUS BELIEFS

Mano Singham

Phi Delta Kappa Educational Foundation
Bloomington, Indiana U.S.A.

Cover design by
Victoria Voelker

Phi Delta Kappa Educational Foundation
408 North Union Street
Post Office Box 789
Bloomington, Indiana 47402-0789
U.S.A.

Printed in the United States of America

Library of Congress Catalog Card Number 00-110371
ISBN 0-87367-830-3

To my mother, Podi,
and my late father, Leo,
who enthusiastically supported
and encouraged me
in all the major decisions of my life.
What I owe to them
cannot be measured
and is a debt
that can never be repaid.

ACKNOWLEDGEMENTS

This book is the result of years of accumulated bits of insight from many different sources. These have come from the writings of others, conversations, casual remarks, and the like. It is impossible to single out all of the people who have influenced me, but there have been many and it has been my privilege to have met and befriended so many of them. Looking back, I am amazed at the numerous acts of kindness and generosity of so many people, some of them strangers. What follows is a very partial list of those people to whom I am indebted, with apologies to the many who have not been explicitly listed.

It is a pleasure to thank my graduate thesis advisor Frank Tabakin (University of Pittsburgh) for teaching me an important lesson — that learning physics should always be fun. He and Loraine Smith Tabakin unhesitatingly came to my rescue at a very critical point in my life and have been a constant source of encouragement throughout. They are true friends.

I also have benefited from the stimulating intellectual atmosphere of Case Western Reserve University and the friendly and collegial attitude of its faculty and staff. They provided me with the ideal environment to start putting ideas together. Interacting with the wonderful students whom I have had the privilege to teach has enlightened me greatly about the learning process. A special word of gratitude must be given to the weekly Public Affairs Luncheons of the university, where I had the privilege (and fun) of discussing a wide variety of topics with knowledgeable and concerned people in many walks of life, from both inside and outside the university. The free and friendly exchange of ideas in an informal setting has broadened my education considerably and has enabled me to see more clearly the underlying unity of knowledge.

It was at these lunches that I also had the good fortune to meet and get to know historian of science Professor Alan Rocke, who read my manuscript and freely and generously gave me valuable advice based on his own deep scholarship and knowledge of the subject.

I am grateful to Jim and Nathalie Andrews, Gordon Brumm, David Farrell, Elizabeth Knoll, David Kolb, Carole Roth, Kesevan Shan, and Mary Zins for reading all or parts of the manuscript and for all of the valuable comments and encouragement they gave during the early stages of writing, and to Donovan Walling and David Ruetschlin of the Phi Delta Kappa Educational Foundation for their invaluable editing of the final manuscript.

Finally, I have to thank my wife, Shermila, and our daughters, Dashi and Ashali, for their willingness to put up with my many hours at the computer typing out the manuscript. Watching Dashi and Ashali grow and learn has been a constant source of inspiration to me. The extended discussions on learning I've had with them as they go through school have taught me so much. They and my sisters, Shanti and Rohini, probably do not fully appreciate how much all the discussions I have had with them have influenced my thinking.

PREFACE

The ideas expressed in this book have been germinating for many years. While it is hard to think of a definite starting point for the process, perhaps the most appropriate one that comes to mind is when, shortly after completing my doctoral degree in physics in 1980, I read Thomas Kuhn's book *The Structure of Scientific Revolutions*. I found that book both exhilarating and disturbing. Exhilarating because the book is extremely well written and argued, and reading such a book is always a pleasure. Disturbing because of its conclusion that there seemed to be no reason to believe that scientific knowledge was leading us closer to The Truth, however one defined that vague concept. Having been attracted to the field of physics because of its promise that it says something real and concrete about the world we live in, and having devoted most of my life to studying the subject, Kuhn's position seemed to whip the rug right out from under my feet. It seemed to imply that I had been following an illusion in thinking that the prolonged study of physics would give me a deep insight into the ultimate *why* questions that all human beings ask themselves about the physical universe and the role we play in it.

Kuhn's book did not make me leave physics, however. I loved the subject too much to consider seriously any other career. But I constantly kept wondering about the ideas discussed in his book, rereading it periodically. With each new reading I gleaned more insights into the history and philosophy of scientific knowledge, but I could see no flaw in his argument or in his conclusions. While the book prompted me to read further into the subject and the works of other authors, I still could find no convincing reasons for rejecting Kuhn's views.

The next blow to my secure worldview came about five years later from the conclusions of another excellent writer, the theoretical physicist John Bell. His own research, as well as his witty and lucid expositions of the views of Albert Einstein on the meaning of quantum mechanics, seemed to cast doubt on another pillar of my belief structure, this relating to whether an objective reality actually existed. This intrigued me and led me to enter a world of ideas on the fundamental nature of physics, an area that had not been much discussed in my formal education or training as a physicist. These ideas, which revolved around whether quantum mechanics was a complete theory and the resulting consequences for whether an objective reality existed, seemed to me to be profound questions that struck at the heart of what we mean by the physical world. Yet not many physicists seemed to be paying much attention to them, and the pressure of other work required me to lay them aside. The questions remained dormant in my mind, unresolved but not forgotten.

Then, in 1992, I became seriously involved with efforts to improve the quality of science education from kindergarten through college. In order to understand what the problems were and how to try and resolve them, I began studying educational methods and techniques. In the process, I was drawn into questions about the nature of knowledge, how it is generated and acquired, and what exactly is going on when we say we learn something. I became slowly aware that learning is a far more subtle and complex process than I initially had assumed.

In researching the various aspects of knowledge, it occurred to me that these questions of truth, objective reality, and knowledge were inextricably linked to one another, and that by treating them as a *coherent whole* one might be able to resolve the conflicts and paradoxes that seemed to exist within each. This attempt at such a synthesis has drawn me into the areas of philosophy of science, education, and epistemology; and this book incorporates strands from all these areas of knowledge. As with any book of this nature, the attempt to answer some questions raises many others that remain unanswered for the present and will have to await further investigation. It is said that a book is never finished, it is only abandoned by its author; and I have decided that it is time for me to abandon mine in its present state.

In formulating the ideas that appear in this book, I have been strongly influenced by many scholarly books and articles, and these I have listed in the bibliography. In particular, anyone who is familiar with Kuhn's classic work will immediately recognize its influence. I also have been influenced by numerous friends, colleagues, and acquaintances whose discussions with me on these subjects have enriched my understanding considerably. It would be impossible to acknowledge each person individually.

The main goal of this book is to create a unified and comprehensive model of the nature of knowledge and its evolution, using the scholarly research that has been available to me. But an important subsidiary goal has been to present the material in a manner that is accessible by nonspecialists. Such an attempt necessarily involves condensing and simplifying the works of others. While I have tried to be as accurate as possible in representing their views and in my statements about the current state of scientific knowledge, some slight distortions must inevitably arise in the process of simplifying some detailed and subtle analyses for the purposes of brevity and in order to make them more accessible to the general reader. I apologize for these distortions and strongly urge the reader to consult the bibliography for deeper analyses on the various topics. I hope that this book provides a doorway to that body of scholarly literature.

This book attempts to reconcile many differing views of science. In doing so, I have had to make generalized statements about what different groups of people (scientists and nonscientists alike) believe. I have not surveyed each group prior to making these statements. My opinions have been formed from my professional associations with colleagues, reading relevant publications, and generally keeping abreast of the public debate on these topics. I have tried to represent them as accurately as possible within that constraint.

But even allowing for that, I recognize that within each group there is a wide diversity of views. Strictly speaking, I should have surrounded each general statement with appropriate qualifications, but this leads to an extraordinarily convoluted writing style. I instead chose to simply leave statements in the form, "Scientists believe . . . ," at the risk of offending those who do not believe any such thing. Because one of the purposes of this book is to create a meaningful dialogue about the nature of knowledge in general and scientific knowledge in particular, perhaps the generalizations themselves will serve to provoke a useful debate by forcing us to clarify exactly what we do and do not believe, and why.

The synthesis that I have attempted about the nature of scientific knowledge is my own creation; but I am well aware that ideas are born, evolve, die, and are reborn in other forms and places so that it is vanity to think that one is the first to think of any given idea. Wherever I have been explicitly aware of the origins of an idea, I have either quoted the source or it is clear from the context. I hope readers of the book will find in it a stimulus to read the writings of the scholars in the various fields that are represented.

TABLE OF CONTENTS

INTRODUCTION:
The Science and Religion Wars*

> The progress of knowledge rigidly requires that no non-physical postulate ever be admitted in connection with the study of physical phenomena. We do not know what is and what is not explicable in physical terms, and the researcher who is seeking explanations must seek physical explanations only.
>
> — George Gaylord Simpson

> All basic types of living things, including man, were made by direct creative acts of God during the Creation Week described in Genesis. Whatever biological changes have occurred since Creation Week have accomplished only changes within the original created kinds.
>
> — Creation Research Society (Numbers 1992, p. 230)

In the spring of 1996 the *Cleveland Plain Dealer* reported on its front page that two physics teachers in a suburban high school had been teaching what is popularly called "creation science" (a biblically based explanation for the origins of life and the universe) in their physics classes for years. Predictably, this caused an uproar locally with angry letters to the editor and the quizzing of school administrators and board members as to how this state of affairs could have gone unnoticed for so long. The flustered school officials responded that the teachers had acted on their own, that this teaching was not school policy; and they called on the teachers to refrain from teaching creation science as part of the science curriculum. The teachers defended their actions by saying that they taught creation science as part of their efforts to instill critical thinking skills in their students by exposing them to alternative models of knowledge. The teachers eventually agreed

---

*Part of this introduction was published in the February 2000 issue of *Phi Delta Kappan* (Singham 2000a) and appears here with permission.

to stop teaching creation science, thus ending a minor skirmish in the long-standing guerilla war that pits the advocates of creationism (or creation science) against the members of the scientific establishment.

There are several noteworthy features about this episode that are characteristic, even though the event itself quickly disappeared over the new horizon. One was that the teaching of creation science had been going on in this school for several years with little or no complaint from either students or their parents. There was little sense that the immediate participants were even aware that they were treading in controversial waters until the newspaper focused attention on them. But as soon as the spotlight was turned on, very strong views were expressed on both sides of the issue.

Supporters of the teachers' actions stated that creation science was a valid alternative worldview of the origin of life and the universe and hence deserved equal treatment with more conventional scientific views. Opponents responded that there was not a shred of scientific evidence to support the creationist point of view and, as such, it was not worthy of inclusion in the science curriculum. Supporters argued that the scientific establishment was imposing only one (its own) view of creation on students and excluding everything else, instead of letting students decide for themselves which belief structure was more plausible. Opponents countered that religious zealots were trying surreptitiously to introduce their religious belief structure into the public schools under the guise of promoting critical thinking in science.

This debate is certainly not new. Ever since science became an independent field of study with its own protocols and methods of generating new knowledge, it has been in conflict with religious beliefs. What is perhaps surprising is the longevity of the science/religion argument. Rather than being resolved or even diminishing with time, the disputes seem to be getting even more pointed, with a hardening of positions over two key issues, one legal and the other epistemological.

The legal issue relates to whether creationism falls within the realm of science or whether it is a religious belief. This is called the *demarcation problem* and involves the question of whether one can formulate unambiguous criteria that successfully distinguish between science and non-science and thus can decide into which category creation science falls.

The epistemological issue hinges on which of two competing theories of the origin of the universe and life is true. On one hand we have the Genesis-inspired models of the creationists, while on the other we have the Big Bang cosmology on the origin of the universe and the Darwinian evolutionary theory on the origins of life, favored by mainstream science.

Legal Issues

In the United States, at least, the question of whether creationism can be adjudicated to be either a religious or scientific belief is not purely academic, because the First Amendment to the Constitution can be invoked to prevent the teaching of creationism in public schools if it is deemed to be a religious belief. Hence it is in the United States that there have been high-profile legal cases debating this very question.

The well-publicized Scopes "monkey trial" in 1925 was technically a defeat for the scientific establishment because a court in Tennessee convicted teacher John Scopes of violating a law banning the teaching of Darwin's theory of evolution in public schools. But while it was a legal defeat for the scientific community, the skill of attorney Clarence Darrow in defending Scopes managed to bring into ridicule biblical theories of the Earth's origin (as propounded by the prosecuting attorney, William Jennings Bryan) and persuade at least elite opinions of that time that the biblical theory of creation was not very credible as a scientific account of the age of the Earth and the origin of species. Thus supporters of Darwinian evolutionary theory achieved a major public relations victory even as they suffered a legal defeat. The explosive growth of science and technology in the middle of this century seemed to consolidate (at least among elite opinion) the feeling that science, and not religion, had the answers to these important questions about the origins of life and the universe.

However, popular support for a biblically based creation model was by no means eliminated by the adverse publicity generated by the Scopes case; and the 1960s saw a dramatic resurgence in creationist views, as well as a shift in their emphasis. Ironically, as we shall see later, this newer version, now bearing the name of "creation science," was even less accommodating of mainstream scientific views than the creationist views advocated by William Jennings Bryan during the Scopes trial. As creation science gained popularity, it was accompanied by attempts to displace evolutionary theory from its dominant position in the education system as *the* explanation for the origin of life. The main arenas for these battles were local school districts, primarily involving the selection of textbooks. Textbook publishers, wary of losing lucrative markets, were under increasing pressure either to eliminate Darwinian evolution theory entirely from textbooks or to tone down its claims to success and offer alternative, implicitly creationist, versions as well. It was inevitable that the conflict would sooner or later spill into the legal arena.

Initial challenges to the theory of evolution took the form of demands that schools and textbook publishers acknowledge that Darwinian evolution was "only a theory" and not a scientific "fact," and hence it should be eliminated from the science curriculum since science was supposed to be concerned only with "facts." (As we shall see later, the meaning of the words "theory" and "fact" are far from self-evident even when applied wholly within the scientific context.) But these initial challenges had only minor success. Schools and teachers could hardly be expected not to say anything at all to students about how life and the universe came to be. Since Darwinian evolution had become accepted by professional scientists as the main organizing principle in understanding the appearance of different life forms, it was inevitable that science textbooks and the training of science teachers would reflect that thinking, albeit in a fairly ad hoc manner.

The paradox was that despite the near universal teaching (in one form or another) of Darwinian evolution in schools, surveys showed a surprising resistance among the general public to key tenets of the theory, especially the one that said humans and apes had common ancestors. As recently as 1988, 38% of college students believed that human life originated in the Garden of Eden (Hively 1988). Feeling that perhaps the reason for this state of affairs was that evolution was not being taught properly, the scientific community planned and implemented a thoroughgoing reform of biology science texts, culminating in the 1960s with the BSCS (Biological Sciences Curriculum Study) textbook series that had evolutionary ideas as a major theme. In these books, there was no escaping the fact that evolution was seen as *the* organizing principle in biology with no viable alternative.

The BSCS series was widely adopted by schools; but it was perceived by creationists as a direct assault by the scientific community on their religious beliefs, and it galvanized them into responding (Numbers 1992). Rather than seek the elimination of the teaching of evolution, a strategy that had not worked earlier, the emphasis now shifted to what was called a "balanced treatment" approach to the teaching of science. Creationists argued that the theory of evolution was just that, a "theory" and not a proven scientific fact. While conceding that this alone did not disqualify it from being taught in schools, they asserted that simple fairness demanded that other theories of life (such as creationism) that also had not been proven should be given equal time in the classroom. Students would then be able to evaluate for themselves which theory made the most sense. Creationists argued that, in addition to meeting the fairness criterion, such a balanced treatment would enhance critical thinking skills in students by encouraging them to think for themselves and to make choices, rather than being told what to believe.

The scientific community countered that this argument was merely a smokescreen in an attempt to introduce religious ideas into the science curriculum. They scoffed at the notion that the creationist model was a *scientific* alternative to the evolutionary model, to be treated on a par with it. They contended that while they respected the religious beliefs of creationists, creationism simply did not meet the criteria to be considered a part of science and thus did not belong in any science curriculum. Despite the opposition of the scientific community, however, the movement for a balanced treatment of creationism and evolution gained ground, culminating in two state legislatures passing laws (Arkansas in 1981 and Louisiana in 1982) requiring that whenever teachers taught "evolution science," they had to give "balanced treatment" to "creation science," which was defined in the Arkansas law in the following way:

> Creation-science includes the scientific evidences and related inferences that indicate:
> (1) Sudden creation of the universe, energy, and life from nothing;
> (2) The insufficiency of mutation and natural selection in bringing about development of all living kinds from a single organism;
> (3) Changes only within fixed limits of originally created kinds of plants and animals;
> (4) Separate ancestry for man and apes;
> (5) Explanation of the earth's geology by catastrophism, including the occurrence of a worldwide flood; and
> (6) A relatively recent inception of the earth and living kinds.

The validity of this law was immediately challenged on constitutional grounds, and the stage was set for yet another legal showdown, one with more significant issues at stake than the Scopes trial. But this time it was creation science that suffered the major legal defeat when in 1982 federal judge William R. Overton ruled that creationism was a religious belief and therefore the Arkansas state law was unconstitutional (*McLean* v. *Arkansas Board of Education* 1982). A similar result occurred for the Louisiana law. In 1987 the U.S. Supreme Court upheld both judges' rulings (*Edwards* v. *Aguillard* 1987). While this was a clear *legal* defeat for the creationist side, it by no means settled the issue in the public mind, as the recent Cleveland episode suggests. The battle for the hearts and minds of the general public is still unresolved.

This book does not seek to re-examine the merits of each side's position on this question. That has been done exhaustively in many forums, often acrimoniously. Instead, I will focus on making explicit the many hidden assumptions that underlie the debate. These assumptions involve the meanings of commonly used words, such as *science, religion, truth, proof, theory, fact, knowledge,* and *reality.* It will be seen that at least part of the reason for the seemingly intractable nature of the conflict is the different interpretations that are given to these words by either side.

The basis on which the federal judge in the Arkansas case arrived at his conclusion is interesting and warrants closer examination, because his ruling raises themes that will recur throughout this book. In his ruling, Judge Overton sought to determine whether the "creation science" assertions fell within the framework of science. In order to do so, he had to address the old demarcation problem of how one decides between what constitutes science and non-science. Guided by the expert testimony of philosopher of science Michael Ruse (1988), the judge stated:

> A descriptive definition was said to be that science is what is "accepted by the scientific community" and is "what scientists do." The obvious implication of this description is that, in a free society, knowledge does not require the imprimatur of legislation in order to become science.
>
> More precisely, the essential characteristics of science are:
> (1) It is guided by natural law;
> (2) It has to be explanatory by reference to natural law;
> (3) It is testable against the empirical world;
> (4) Its conclusions are tentative, i.e. are not necessarily the final word; and
> (5) It is falsifiable.
>
> Creation science... fails to meet these essential characteristics. [It] asserts a sudden creation "from nothing." Such a concept is not science because it depends upon a supernatural intervention which is not guided by natural law. It is not explanatory by reference to natural law, is not testable and is not falsifiable.

The judge's formulation of what can be considered to constitute science is one that is commonly held and seems at first glance to be reasonably self-evident. At its core, it asserts that there is an "empirical" (external and objective) world, that the merits of theories can be evaluated by seeing how well their predictions agree with this world, and that scientific theories must be falsifiable. In later chapters, I will examine all these assertions in some detail and find that justifying them is not as simple as it may seem.

Creationist Models

The interesting thing about the creationism debate is the fact that it is a fiercely partisan argument with both sides convinced of the rightness of their own cause and the error of the opponents. Even giving the conflict a name is not without controversy. For example, the debate frequently is framed as "Science versus Creationism," but this commonly used label can be misleading and prejudicial. It seems to assume that science and creationism occupy different and *mutually exclusive* spheres in the world of knowledge and so carries the subtle implication that to be a creationist is to not be scientific and vice versa. This characterization would be hotly contested by many creationists who view themselves as scientists and view their beliefs as falling under the umbrella of science. They would prefer the debate to be framed as whether the theory of evolution by natural selection (as proposed by Charles Darwin) is correct as the *sole* explanation of how the different life forms appeared or whether an active Creator also was involved in life's creation, guiding the process.

Even to lump one side under the single label "creationists" is to do them an injustice and to ignore the facts that 1) there is a broad range of views encompassed by this label and 2) there are furious internal disagreements among them as to which version is best. (In his 1992 book, *The Creationists*, Ronald Numbers carefully examines the differences between the various schools of creationist thought, their history and evolution, and the personalities behind them.) In describing the various forms of creationism, it is helpful to rank them from their strongest to the weakest. I should hasten to add that the descriptions of "weak" and "strong" forms are used here not in the sense of degrees of robustness, but as they are sometimes used in describing scientific theories. A weak form of a theory is one in which only the barest restrictions are imposed, allowing for a great deal of flexibility in usage and interpretation. A strong form, by contrast, is one in which there are many restrictions, reduced flexibility, and strict guidelines on how the theory is to be interpreted.

The strong version of creationism is called *flood geology* (Whitcomb and Morris 1961) and is the version most properly associated with the commonly used label "creation science." Adherents believe that the universe, life, humans, and other major species were created more or less whole by a divine Creator within the last ten thousand years or so. Some allow for the possibility of a much older but lifeless earth, but all insist that the first formation of life and humans (Adam and Eve) occurred in an Edenic Restoration created in six 24-hour days somewhere between 4000 and 8000 B.C. They also assert the historicity of a global (Noah's) flood around 3000 B.C., which formed all the fossils that are now being discovered. Among creationists, the flood geologists tend to be the ones most likely to take the Genesis story in the Bible as a literal record of actual historical events. They are thus forced to reject all standard scientific interpretations of geologic evidence giving a greater antiquity for the earth and biological evidence for evolution of life.

The moderate form of creationism is what is known as the "gap" or "ruin and reconstruction" theory. This allows for a very old, unspecified age of the universe in which matter was first created, followed by non-human life and the formation of fossils. This creation process could have involved multiple cataclysms and creations and is flexible enough to accommodate most geologic evidence. But when it comes to the first appearance of humans, the model becomes very similar to that of the flood geologists. In 4004 B.C there is an Edenic Restoration with the first humans, Adam and Eve, created in six 24-hour days, followed in 2348 B.C. by Noah's flood, which in this model need not be a global flood but could be a local phenomenon.

The weak form of creationism has an even more flexible structure and is known as the "day-age" model. This allows for a very old, unspecified age of the universe in which matter was first created, followed by life, the formation of fossils, and finally human beings. Noah's flood also was a historical event in this model, but it could be a local phenomenon. All of these events have unspecified dates that can accommodate values obtained using the standard dating techniques of science. The six "days" of creation in the Genesis story are interpreted metaphorically as representing long but indeterminate periods of time, whence comes the name of this model. Adam and Eve and the garden of Eden story also are interpreted metaphorically and not as actual historical events.

The strong, moderate, and weak forms of creationism all insist that the various forms of life that exist on earth did not simply evolve into being through natural laws but were deliberate acts of creation by an active Creator. This does not mean that adherents of these three models disallow evolutionary change altogether. They concede that changes do occur over time. The commonplace fact that children are not mere copies of their parents provides undeniable evidence for some degree of change. What is asserted is that such changes can occur over only a restricted range. The main categories of life (known as "kinds") appeared as a result of deliberate acts of creation by a divine Creator and not as a result of one form evolving into another. What constitutes a "kind" is not precisely specified (it is vaguely similar to a species), but there is little disagreement about what is not allowed. Birds and reptiles are of different "kinds," thus ruling out the evolutionary idea that birds evolved from reptiles. Similarly, humans and apes are of different "kinds," ruling out ape ancestors for humankind. So while some of these models are compatible with geological and cosmological theories for the *physical* origins of the universe, they are all in flat contradiction to conventional biological explanations for the origins of key life forms.

One other form of creationism requires special mention, and that is what I call the *superweak* form, also called "intelligent design" (Behe 1996). This model is not concerned with questions involving timetables. Rather than proposing a specific mechanism for the appearance of matter and life in the universe, superweak creationists instead focus on the weaknesses of evolutionary theory. They examine the evidence in support of evolution and find it wanting (Johnson 1991). They argue that there is little evidence for the idea that a steady accumulation of micromutations could evolve into the huge macromutations required to make the transition from reptiles to birds or from apes to humans. They also argue that it is statistically impossible for the various species currently in existence to have evolved from one to another by purely natural causes, even within the very long timeframes currently set by science for these processes. They thus *infer* that some form of divine guidance (a Creator) had to be present and actively involved to nudge things along at critical moments in order for us to be able to explain the appearance of life in all its present forms within the 15 or so billion years that science tells us the universe has been in existence.

The merits of these four differing models are the subject of debate within the creationist world and can generate considerable passion, not unlike disagreements within the scientific community over different theories. It also should be appreciated that these internal debates within the creationist movement are not based on religious texts alone but also use standard scientific knowledge and methods to argue the merits of the respective points of view.

If there is one common thread that all creationists share, it is that the world as we know it now is too complex and subtle to have come about without the active and repeated intervention of an external agent or a deity, acting outside the laws of science. It is this unifying belief (rather than any specific model or religious tradition) that I will characterize as the "creationist" point of view. Formulated this way, we see that creationist beliefs are not reserved purely for some narrow sectarian group but incorporate major elements of mainstream Christianity, Judaism, Hinduism,

Islam, and other theistic religions. They differ only in their beliefs about the extent and nature of this divine intervention. In a poll conducted in March 2000, 68% of Americans said that "it was possible simultaneously to believe in evolution and also that God created humans and guided their development."

The last model that should be mentioned is one in which the Creator is a sort of prime mover who creates the universe and all its laws of evolution at one instant at the beginning of the universe but never intervenes thereafter, allowing the universe to evolve in the manner revealed by science. This model has a Creator in it, but is not creationist as defined above because there is no subsequent intervention at all in any form to change the natural course of events.

It is important to re-emphasize that even the more fundamentalist creationists do not reject all scientific knowledge or the scientific method. They do not invoke acts of divine creation cavalierly to explain everything, as is sometimes erroneously suggested by their opponents. They tend to take a minimalist approach to divine intervention, invoking it in only a few rare instances when they feel that conventional scientific explanations are either implausible or flatly contradict a key tenet of the Bible. They claim that the biblical account is a model (or hypothesis) that is consistent with data from, say, geology and paleontology. It is just that they disagree with most geologists and paleontologists on how that data is analyzed and interpreted. While creationists do not use the Bible as their sole authority for understanding natural phenomena, they do use the information in the Bible as an integral part of their worldview. This makes their model more restrictive and less flexible than those within conventional science that do not use the Bible as part of their theoretical framework. However, the creationists are laying their beliefs on the line. A rejection of their model would force them to become unbelievers because it would imply a rejection of the Bible itself. It is not a gamble they take lightly, and so the vehemence with which they argue in support of their position should come as no surprise.

The Nature of the Conflict

The scientific establishment, conversely, starts with the assumption that all natural phenomena should be explainable by natural laws that can be discovered using the methods of science. It does not allow for even one deviation from these natural laws. Miracles, which by definition are direct contradictions of the workings of natural laws, have no place in this framework. I will characterize this as the "naturalist" point of view, instead of "scientific," in order to avoid the subtle implication that creationism, simply by definition, lies outside the realm of science. So in this essay the debate will be cast as creationism versus naturalism. I will reserve the word "science" for the body of knowledge held in common by the majority of professional scientists (typically working in academic and research settings) and as represented by their official professional organizations, published in professional journals, and the methods used to acquire this knowledge.

Like the differences within the creationist camp, there is a similar divergence of views within the naturalist camp involving spirited debates over interpretation of facts and theories. One such example is the disagreement over whether biological evolution proceeded relatively uniformly over time with a steady progression of minute changes leading to the creation of new species or whether there were long periods of stability punctuated by bursts of rapid change. There also are disagreements among cosmologists over the precise age of the universe and its constituent stars and over the composition of the universe and its large-scale structure. Just like much of the internal creationist debate over conflicting viewpoints, the discussion among naturalists involves weighing the importance of various pieces of evidence and the inferences that can legitimately be drawn from them.

The naturalist community typically tends to regard creationist beliefs as unscientific because those beliefs require that all scientific knowledge be consistent (to some extent) with the Bible. Because science rejects any form of textual infallibility and views all knowledge as provisional and subject to testing, beliefs based on a text automatically put creationism outside the pale of science. The naturalists tend to view creationists as religious zealots who reflexively reject all scientific knowledge that does not agree with their particular interpretation of history as revealed by the Bible.

Creationists are no less scathing in their view of naturalism. They see evolution by Darwinian natural selection as an extremely weak theory that fails to meet all the tests that are normally required for any successful scientific theory, and that it is only by using its hegemonic power, instead of scientific argument, that the scientific establishment manages to keep creationism out of textbooks and the schools (Gish 1981). They argue that they believe in creationism because evolution, in all its variants, is a falsified theory and creationism is the only viable alternative. They assert that those opposed to creationism are atheists who are imposing their own "religious" worldview (atheism) on students under the guise of science. Creationists view naturalists as zealots who reject all scientific knowledge that does not agree with their particular interpretation of history as revealed by Darwinian natural selection.

To the casual observer this conflict seems to be about deciding between two fairly straightforward, but dissonant, propositions. On the one hand is the view that both creation science and evolution are unproven theories and that simple fairness requires that either they both be taught or both be omitted from the school science curriculum. On the other hand, the argument is made that creation science is a religion-based belief while evolution is not, and thus the establishment clause of the First Amendment to the Constitution justifies the exclusion of the former from the public school curriculum and the inclusion of the latter.

When one looks at the internal debates within the naturalist and creationist camps, one is struck by the civility of the discussion that takes place. Points are raised and debated, evidence is examined and rejected, theories rise and fall, mostly (though not always) in a spirit of collegiality. However, this happy picture changes dramatically when the two camps confront each other. Then each side tends to close ranks and present a unified front to the other. An unwillingness to see the subtleties of the others' belief structures is the rule, rather than the exception. Caricaturing opponents' views and then subjecting them to ridicule is a common tactic. The debate is frequently mean-spirited, using the unfortunate (but common) tactic of comparing the worst and weakest aspects of the opponents' point of view with the best of one's own.

While the intensity and ferocity of the creationists' attacks on the naturalist viewpoint can be explained (if not excused) by realizing that they have placed a fundamental belief structure on the line, the equally fierce response of the established naturalist community is a little harder to understand. After all, scientists proudly acknowledge that all knowledge is provisional and that they are not irrevocably committed to any one belief structure. But there is something about the creationist claims that seem to strike a nerve in the scientific community, causing some members to lash out in response. Perhaps the scientific community feels that they alone represent the last line of defense in the fight against irrationalism and its consequent evils and that to concede any ground to the forces that challenge the authority of scientific knowledge (as defined by the scientists themselves) would be like allowing a hole in the dike of rationalism — a prelude to unleashing a flood of irrational nonsense. Both sides seem to view this battle as one with momentous implications, that anything short of total victory is unthinkable. Hence we have a "take no prisoners" attitude, using scorn, ridicule, parody, and all of the other unintellectual weapons at each sides' disposal.

The fact that both sides believe fiercely in the rightness of their positions should give us a clue that the underlying issues involving science and religion are not really that simple. In fact, they do involve subtle and complex questions, drawing on knowledge from many disciplines. It often is said that politics makes strange bedfellows, but perhaps nowhere can stranger bedfellows be found than in the controversies surrounding science and religion. Scientists, theologians, creationists, postmodernists, social constructivists, feminists, multiculturalists, philosophers, and histori-

ans of science all play key, and often surprising, roles in this con-
tentious debate.

Disentangling the Combatants

To understand how these strange coalitions get formed, a good
place to start is to look at the discussions of scientific literacy that
periodically occur among elite opinion makers. There are three
features of such discussions that are entirely predictable.

The first is that everyone will lament the sorry state of scientific literacy in the United States and predict dire consequence if
this situation is not improved.

The second feature is the inevitable listing of all the deplorable
things that the general public believes (such as aliens, alternative
medicine, astrology, psychokinesis, superstitions, and the like)
and that allegedly contribute to this illiteracy. For convenience, I
will lump all of these alternative beliefs under the label of "fringe
beliefs," not because they are held by only a few people (some of
them may represent a majority of the population) but because
they lie on the fringes of elite opinion. These fringe beliefs are
considered disreputable and labeled with such pejoratives as
"pseudo-science" or "non-science" or "nonsense."

The third predictable feature is harder to observe because, like
the dog that did not bark in the night in the Sherlock Holmes
story, it involves noticing what is not said. No one raises the question as to what fundamental difference, if any, exists between
these supposedly non- (or even anti-) science fringe beliefs and
those of mainstream religions. And it is this silent issue that must
be confronted if we are to understand the often bizarre coalitions
that form and re-form around the science-religion issue.

In the triangle formed by science, mainstream religion, and
fringe beliefs, it is the conflict between science and fringe beliefs
that usually is the source of the most heated, acrimonious, and
public debate. The other two relationships (between science and
mainstream religion and between mainstream religion and fringe
beliefs) usually are ignored. But the relationships among all three

knowledge structures have to be examined if we are to make any sense of the problem, because it ultimately boils down to two key questions: Is it possible to set up a hierarchy of belief structures with science and mainstream religions at the top (and thus "respectable") and with fringe beliefs at the bottom (and thus disreputable)? What makes elite opinion makers feel that science is compatible with mainstream religious beliefs but incompatible with fringe beliefs?

Part of the confusion in dealing with these questions arises from trying to lump everything under the label of either *science* or *religion*. Following the suggestion of theologian Langston Gilkey (Numbers 1992), it is perhaps more enlightening to split each of the two belief structures into two subgroups (elite and popular science, elite and popular religion) and to look at the relationships between the resulting four subgroups.

Elite science encompasses the consensus belief structures of the scientific establishment, as represented in the departments of science at universities and research institutes and published in mainstream scientific journals. Members of this group have a fundamental naturalist belief in the idea that every physical phenomenon must have a scientific explanation, with no arbitrariness allowed. The eminent paleontologist George Gaylord Simpson (who had some personal reservations about the belief that everything in the universe can be explained naturalistically) captured the essence of the naturalistic position when he said, "the progress of knowledge rigidly requires that *no non-physical postulate ever be admitted* in connection with the study of physical phenomena. We do not know what is and what is not explicable in physical terms, and the researcher who is seeking explanations must seek physical explanations only" (Simpson 1944, p. 76, emphasis added).

Popular science, on the other hand, includes people's widely held beliefs in superstitions, astrology, magic, witchcraft, psychokinesis, extrasensory perception, and the like, all of which can be grouped under what I have called fringe beliefs. Such people view as quaint the notion that everything must have a scientific explanation. They have no difficulty in believing that there are ext-raphysical entities capable of violating the laws of science at will.

Elite religion represents those views held by theologians of mainstream religions. In the theistic religions this view holds that while a creator exists, the creator does not directly intervene (or at least only rarely) to change the course of everyday events, thus violating scientific laws. Changes are usually achieved indirectly by changing the minds of people and causing them to act in dif-ferent and better ways.

Popular religion, on the other hand, believes in a personal God, a creator who can and does intervene when and if the creator sees fit, and thus can be induced to intervene to change the course of everyday events by prayer and other supplications. Fundamental-ist believers in most major religions tend to fall into this category.

So who is fighting with whom? Popular science and popular religion generally have no problems with each other (and I group them under the umbrella label of fringe beliefs). After all, both groups have no difficulty in accepting the occurrence of phenom-ena that defy scientific explanations. This does not mean that they always agree; for example, fundamentalist Christians are ad-amantly opposed to witchcraft. But such disagreements deal with issues of moral right and wrong and good versus evil and have nothing to do with the issue being addressed here of whether it is possible to have events that violate scientific laws.

Similarly, elite and popular religions also tend not to have open conflicts because major religions tend to gather both viewpoints under their umbrellas. The mass base tends to adopt popular reli-gious views about an interventionist deity, while the elite believes that God works in indirect and subtle ways that are not easily attributable.

Elite science and popular science, on the other hand, have had a long history of conflict, ever since science became (around the time of Galileo) an established field of study with its own proto-cols for evidence and establishing truths. Even now the constant calls for increasing scientific literacy are a symptom of the scien-tific community's exasperation with the fact that, after so many years of mass science education, large numbers of people still believe in all kinds of things that the scientific community views as wholly irrational. For example, fairly recent surveys show that 55% of American teenagers believe that "astrology works" (Hively 1988).

The nature of all three of the above relationships have been stable over the years. What is interesting is the dramatic change in the fourth relationship, the one between elite science and elite religion. In the early days of science, this relationship was one of hostility, as scientific knowledge grew and rapidly dethroned religion as the source of authoritative knowledge about the world. From the days of the Copernican revolution and Galileo through Darwin's publication of *On the Origin of Species,* elite religion battled the scientific community to see which worldview would dominate.

The relationship between elite science and elite religion nowadays is dramatically different and can be characterized by the Cold War concept of *peaceful coexistence.* In its political context, this term referred to the recognition of separate spheres of influence over which each side in the Cold War held unquestioned supremacy. This avoided endless border skirmishes that might precipitate a major conflict.

The nature of the remaining two relationshipes (between elite religion and popular science and between elite science and and popular religion) are easier to appreciate because they represent high-profile conflicts. The former was the basis of the Inquisition and other violent attempts to stamp out perceived offenses (such as witchcraft) against religious orthodoxy. The latter is what currently is popularly understood as the conflict between science and creationism.

The Two Worlds Model

In between these two extremes of naturalism and creationism seems to lie a middle ground. The philosophical basis for this can be called the "two worlds model." The physical realm, comprising all phenomena accessible by the senses, belongs to the world of science; while the spiritual realm, dealing with moral and ethical questions and with the soul and the afterlife, belongs to the world of religion. This formulation is captured in a statement by the council of the prestigious National Academy of Sciences, which says, "[R]eligion and science are *separate and mutually exclusive realms* of human thought whose presentation in the same context leads to misunderstanding of both scientific theory and religious belief" (National Academy of Sciences Committee on Science and Creationism 1984, p. 6, emphasis added).

Most noncombatants in the science-religion wars subscribe to some form of this statement and thus see no conflict between scientific and religious belief structures. This group is composed of a large number of people, scientists and nonscientists alike, who are respectful of science and its accomplishments but also believe in a deity and are active members of churches, temples, and mosques. Such people view the creation narratives in their respective religious texts as figurative and metaphorical and not as records of actual historical events. Such people also tend to view the periodic legal and political skirmishes between the creationist and naturalist camps as the work of overzealous extremists, both religious and scientific, who are attempting to mix together things that should properly stay separate.

But is this "middle ground" viewpoint intellectually robust enough to achieve amity between the scientific and religious worldviews? In other words, do religious views about the workings of the world have a *fundamental* conflict with known scientific laws? Or does this middle ground survive by not asking awkward questions?

One awkward question that is avoided deals with the miraculous events that are central to every theistic religious tradition and that seem directly to violate the laws of science. Are they purely the result of natural laws (of which we may be currently unaware) thus ceasing to be miracles in any meaningful sense of the word, or are they singular events that occur in direct contradiction to natural laws?

Take, for example, the well-known biblical story of the parting of the Red Sea (or the Sea of Reeds). In the orthodox religious view this is a miracle pure and simple, an act that occurs in clear contradiction to natural laws. So does it belong only to the world of religion? Yet it is an event that is supposed to have occurred in the physical world, so it also should belong to the world of science. How can the National Academy of Sciences' sharp distinction between the spiritual and physical world be sustained? One solution is to reject the idea that the parting of the Red Sea ever occurred as described, thus denying it historical status. Another is to look for evidence that some unusual but wholly natural combination of causes resulted in something that seemed to be miraculous to the naive observer of that time. The key consequence of both these explanations is to remove the event from the realm of the miraculous. The historical evolution of knowledge has been precisely in this direction, replacing "miraculous" occurrences with scientific explanations.

But can *every* event that is commonly believed to be miraculous be explained away in this manner? The committed naturalist would argue that this must be so, otherwise the entire framework of science will collapse. The scientific establishment starts with the assumption that all natural phenomena should be explainable by natural laws that can be discovered using the methods of science. It does not allow for even one deviation from these natural laws. Miracles, which by definition are direct contradictions of the workings of natural laws, have no place in this framework.

The evolutionary geneticist Richard C. Lewontin says it clearly and bluntly: "We cannot live simultaneously in a world of natural causation and of miracles, for if one miracle can occur, there is no limit" (Godfrey 1983). His point is well taken. If the scientific community concedes even one miraculous event, then how can it credibly contest the view that the world (and all its fossilized relics) were created in one instant just six thousand years ago? Robert Park, the director of public affairs for the American Physical Society, goes even further when he says that "to attribute natural events to supernatural forces is not merely lazy, it defines anti-science" (Park 1996).

Although these comments were specifically aimed at creationists, they undermine traditional mainstream religions as well. If there is to be no divine intervention at all, what is left for religion? Is it just a system of beliefs that have no tangible consequences whatsoever? In his book, *The End of Science* (1996), John Horgan quotes cosmologist Stephen Hawking asking rhetorically, "What place, then, for a creator?" There is no place, was Hawking's own reply; a final theory would exclude God from the universe and with him all mystery. Hawking "hoped to root mysticism, vitalism, creationism from their last refuge, the origin of the universe."

Another awkward question that is avoided is that while we can readily see that the physical world exists, is there any tangible evidence that a moral/ethical/spiritual world also exists?

If the answer is no (so that the existence of the moral/ethical/ spiritual world is to be simply believed and not experienced in any way), that means its existence does not have any consequences that affect the physical world. Then of what use is this other world? What would be the point of believing in a deity if the spiritual world occupied by the deity could have no influence whatsoever on the physical world we actually live in? This answer seems to imply that we can dispense entirely with the spiritual world, a position that is surely not the intention of those advocating the two worlds model.

If the answer is yes, how can we still maintain the clear distinction between the two worlds? After all, tangible evidence is something that belongs to the physical world, and so evidence for the existence of a spiritual world must imply that the two worlds overlap.

In fact, it quickly becomes clear that this middle ground that treats "religion and science [as] separate and mutually exclusive realms of human thought" contains a basic internal contradiction. The middle ground seems to start by saying that there is a self-contained world of natural laws and another self-contained world of spiritual laws. But then it goes on to imply (because moral and ethical values presumably influence human behavior) that these two worlds *do* overlap, which means that they are not self-contained after all.

Why is it that this middle ground is so popular and its shaky foundations relatively immune from close questioning? It is possible that, wearied by the historical baggage of such conflicts as those involving Galileo and Darwin, the elite scientific community has reached an unspoken agreement with mainstream religions that they will not attack each other. The physical/spiritual distinction provides a useful escape route for both groups. Pope John Paul II's statement in 1996 that "fresh knowledge" (which he failed to specify) "leads to recognition of the theory of evolution as more than just a hypothesis" can be viewed as further consolidating this alliance. The Pope did reserve some area for religion by emphasizing that "if the human body has its origins in living material which pre-exists it, the spiritual soul is immediately created by God," thus showing that he, too, is an advocate of the "two worlds" model endorsed by the National Academy of Sciences (Tagliabue 1996).

Thus elite science is allowed to interpret the physical world while elite religions interpret the spiritual world, and both sides agree to not wander onto each other's turf. This tacit agreement allows them to combine forces and attack those who brazenly mix the two worlds together, such as those who believe in creation science as well as those who believe in other unorthodoxies, such as astrology, witchcraft, New Age mysticism, and the like. For example, in the 1981 Arkansas "balanced treatment" case, the witnesses against the law mandating that creationism also be taught in schools were from mainstream religions as well as from the scientific establishment.

The Creationist Counterattack on the Two Worlds Model

Creationists, understandably, are unhappy with the development of this alliance because it makes them vulnerable to attack on two fronts. Continuing with the war metaphor, they look on the deal as appeasement by the elite religionists who have been duped by the scientific elite into thinking they have achieved a long-term peace, when what the elite religionists have really done is to lose the war by allowing the scientific community complete hegemony over the physical world.

Nowadays elite religion has tacitly (if not openly) conceded the understanding of the physical world to science, reserving for itself the moral/ethical/spiritual realm. The creationists argue that the elite religionists' strategy of retreating to the moral and ethical sphere for their realm results in an extremely weak position that can be easily overrun by the advancing scientific hordes. After all, it is quite possible that advances in neurobiology may be able to pinpoint specific areas in the brain that are the source of moral and ethical impulses and spiritual feelings. Scientists even may be able to locate which neurons trigger good and bad impulses or generate moral decisions.

Creationists realize that such developments will result in the total subjugation of religious beliefs to scientific hegemony. Thus it should not be surprising if some of the most incisive critiques of the naturalist view have come from creationists, who see in it a real threat to their own religious belief structure. Rather than try to fight border skirmishes with science to eke out a larger sphere of influence for religion, these creationists have gone for broke, waging an all-out counterattack on elite science.

The attack has been two-pronged. On one front, they try to drive a wedge between elite science and elite religion by arguing that the scientific and religious worldviews are incompatible at a fundamental level and both cannot be believed simultaneously. Some creationists have sought to win back elite religion to their side by pointing out to followers of mainstream religions that their beliefs also are undermined if the claims of the naturalists to sole authority for knowledge of the physical world are allowed to pass unchallenged. They argue that the very same arguments that are used to assert that creationism is incompatible with science also can be used to argue that mainstream religious beliefs are inconsequential, because the spiritual world has no influence whatsoever on the physical world. In other words, the creationists argue that all the naturalists who reject creationism as being

either irrelevant or wrong are actually (though not openly) imply-
ing the same thing about mainstream religious beliefs as well.

Phillip Johnson, a creationist, recently wrote a book titled
Darwin on Trial (1991) that makes the, by now, familiar claims
that Darwinism is a poor theory both on logical grounds ("survival of the fittest" as a mechanism for change is tautologous and
lacks any predictive power) and on evidentiary grounds (the evidence is sparse for the existence of intermediate forms of life
between species, and the rate at which micromutations can occur
is not rapid enough to explain the current diversity in life forms).
But he goes on to make the explicit charge that beliefs in evolution and a creator are fundamentally incompatible.

The response to Johnson's book was fierce. Paleontologist
Stephen Jay Gould responded with a vitriolic review in *Scientific
American* magazine (Gould 1992, p. 118). After responding to
the logical and evidentiary arguments, which he had encountered
many times before, he then directed his attention to the claim that
beliefs in science and God are mutually exclusive. It was clear
that Johnson's charge had stung. For example, Gould says, "Either
half my colleagues are enormously stupid, or else the science of
Darwinism is fully compatible with conventional religious beliefs
— and equally compatible with atheism." Or later, "To say it for
all my colleagues and for the umpteenth millionth time . . . science simply cannot (by its legitimate methods) adjudicate the
issue of God's possible superintendence of nature. We neither
affirm it nor deny it; we simply can't comment on it as scientists.
. . . Science can work only with naturalistic explanations; it can
neither affirm nor deny other types of actors (like God) in other
spheres (the moral realm, for example)."

Gould also states that "[Science and religion] should not conflict because science treats factual reality, while religion struggles
with moral reality," and asserts that there is a "consensus that science and religion are separate and equally valuable," both of
which are reformulations of the National Academy of Sciences'
"two realms" statement. The key point that Gould does not
address is the nature of the "moral reality" he refers to. If by this

he means that religious beliefs can influence our behavior, then that resulting behavior must be part of the *physical* "factual reality," and hence the two realities are not separate.

Gould is certainly correct when he asserts that many scientists are also religious believers. Surveys conducted in 1996 and 1998 found that about 40% of scientists believe in a personal God as defined by the statement "a God in intellectual and affirmative communication with . . . to whom one may pray in expectation of receiving an answer." Despite the explosive growth in science this century, this figure of 40% has remained stable since previous surveys done in 1914 and 1933 (Larson and Witham 1997, p. 435; Larson and Witham 1999, p. 89). The figure would undoubtedly be much higher if belief in a non-personal God (some sort of prime mover who acted only through natural laws) were included as well.

There are two interesting features about Gould's review. One is the extreme harshness of the response. Gould is one of the more open-minded of well-known scientists and usually understanding of heterodox views. Creationists frequently use his frank views on the ambiguities and problems of evolution to attack the theory, much to his chagrin. But here he unequivocally lays down the scientific party line against creationism. The second interesting feature is that instead of countering Johnson's views with careful arguments, he responds by simply asserting that the two belief systems must be compatible because many scientists are also religious people. Gould seems to be saying that his position, that science and religion are compatible, must be correct simply because he and many other scientists believe it to be compatible.

In a subsequent book (Gould 1999), Gould expands on this position, trying to further make the case for the "two worlds" model. He reserves all explanations for physical phenomena to the realm of science (and explicitly rules out the possibility of any miraculous events) while leaving the moral and ethical realm for religion. But he still does not address the awkward issue of the source of moral and ethical feelings. Do they originate within the brain and achieve their effects by commands that originate from the brain? If so, surely they lie within the realm of science because the brain is a part of the physical world and thus subject to the investigations of science. However, if moral and ethical feelings transcend the brain, then how can they have any influence on people?

Evolutionary biologist Francisco Ayala (the president of the American Association for the Advancement of Science in 1994, Ayala was called as an expert witness against the creationist position at the 1981 Arkansas trial) also tries Gould's approach of arguing that science and religion must be compatible because famous intellectuals think they are. Whereas Gould points to the religious beliefs of scientists, Ayala looks for support to the scientific views of famous theologians. Speaking at a symposium, "Antiscience/Anti-evolution," he examined what Saint Augustine and Thomas Aquinas had to say about the Bible and creation. Ayala concluded, "The point is that the two greatest thinkers of Christianity could find no reason based on the Bible that species could [not] find their origin in causes other than God." He goes on to quote two Popes (Leo XIII and John Paul II) to the effect that the Bible should not be interpreted literally or serve as a source of scientific understanding ("Evolution and the Bible," 1995, p. 5).

Both Gould and Ayala seem to be arguing that because eminent scientists and eminent theologians do not see a conflict between science and religion, there is no such conflict. But all it might mean is that such people *want* to maintain peace between elite science and elite religion and are not keen on provoking a split.

Creationists, who have been the targets of this alliance between elite religion and elite science, have no such interest in papering over any fundamental conflict that might exist between the two. In this they receive support from an unlikely source, biologist Richard Dawkins. Dawkins is a fervent advocate of Darwinian natural selection, the very theory that creationists love to hate. He has spent a great deal of time and effort to refute the claims of creationists that it is highly improbable that natural selection could have led to the diversity, complexity, and sophistication of present-day life forms (Dawkins 1996). But Dawkins joins forces with Johnson in pouring scorn on the "two worlds" model of the National Academy of Sciences, calling it "a cowardly cop-out. I think it's an attempt to woo the sophisticated theological lobby and to get them into our camp and put the creationists into another camp. It's good politics. But it's intellectually disreputable" (Larson and Witham 1999, p. 91).

The second front opened by the creationists in their war with elite science is a direct attack on the very foundations of the scientific worldview, which is that science is the sole source of authoritative knowledge about the physical world. And in this attack creationists also have found some other unlikely allies, namely philosophers and historians of science and postmodern social constructivists of knowledge.

As we shall see later in the book, philosophers of science, following in the tradition of Thomas Kuhn (1970), Karl Popper (1962), Imre Lakatos (1986), and Paul Feyerabend (1993), have long tried to understand the basis on which scientific knowledge derives its success and authority. It seems plausible that this success can come about only because the methods of science are leading toward the truth. But the notions of truth and objective reality have been extraordinarily difficult to pin down. Although these philosophers of science are, by and large, supporters of science and admirers of its achievements, they have concluded that there is no definitive reason to believe that scientific progress is leading to the truth about the physical world — or even that there is such a thing as the truth or objective reality.

Postmodern philosophers have expanded on this last point. Social constructivists have argued that all knowledge, including scientific knowledge, is filtered and interpreted through the lens of the observer and is thus inevitably colored by that lens. What this means is that when I directly experience something through my senses (I see a pencil, say), I make sense of that experience using my prior knowledge (what a pencil looks like, feels like, and does) and embed the new experience in my existing knowledge framework, modifying that framework in the process. Each person does the same thing; but because each person's history is different, his or her understanding of the same phenomenon also will differ. The unfiltered truth about a pencil (independent of any particular observer's interpretation) is thus impossible to discern. The best we can hope for is to negotiate a shared meaning so that we can communicate with one another.

Some social constructivists argue that modern scientific knowledge is the product of the (primarily male and Western) people who were involved in its creation and that there might be equally valid alternative scientific worldviews, depending on the perspective of the people who engage in it (Bloor 1976). Thus science cannot claim that its knowledge structure is *objective* and *unique*, and this has led to the discussion of possible alternatives, such as feminist science and multicultural science, in contrast to the present "orthodox" science (Tuana 1989).

Scientists employ a version of positivism (the view that the only things we can talk about are those that we can show to exist by making measurements) to both understand and interpret scientific theories (especially difficult ones, such as quantum mechanics) and to attack fringe beliefs and creationism (because those beliefs involve phenomena that elude systematic observation). Taking a leaf from positivist science, however, radical social constructivists have argued that there can be no objective reality at all because one can never detect its existence independently of the interpretations of the observer. This illustrates another of the many ironies in the science wars in which one of the pillars of the scientific worldview (positivism) is used to undermine another pillar (the belief in an objective reality). The existence or non-existence of an objective reality is a key issue that will be explored repeatedly later.

Some creationists have used the arguments of all these groups to aver that elite science, rather than being the imposing body of knowledge its supporters claim it to be, has feet of clay and that its claim to sole authoritative knowledge about the physical world is unjustified. In particular, creationists assert that the views of elite science on the issue of evolution should not be taken unquestioningly.

The scientific community has been somewhat flummoxed by the wide-ranging nature of the criticisms it has received. The assault against its authority by an unexpected convergence of this diverse group of creationists, philosophers of science, postmodernists, social constructivists, feminists, and multiculturalists (groups that share little in common other than their skepticism of the scientific community's claims to have special knowledge about the physical world) — coupled with the refusal of large segments of the public to give up their beliefs in astrology and the like — has caused considerable despair within the scientific community. They decry what they see as widespread scientific illiteracy being exploited to create a growing antiscience sentiment.

The response to this situation by the more moderate members of the elite science community has been to call for more investment in science education in order to improve science literacy. This group feels that the problem arises because of popular misunderstanding and ignorance about the nature of the scientific enterprise. They believe that if the public really understood what science is and how its knowledge is acquired, they would be more supportive of science and skeptical of these alternative beliefs.

However, the more militant members of elite science see a more sinister antiscience conspiracy at work and have launched a vigorous counter-attack. In the vanguard have been Paul Gross and Norman Levitt. In their book, *Higher Superstition* (1994), they rail against philosophers, feminists, postmodernists, and all of the other people within the academy (whom they dub the "academic left") whom they feel are deliberately undermining the authority of science in an attempt to dethrone science from its position of prestige within the academy. Their polemic is a bitter and often mean-spirited attack on anyone whom they see as an enemy of science.

They followed this by convening a conference in New York in 1995 titled *The Flight from Science and Reason* (Gross, Levitt, and Lewis 1996). About 200 academics were invited to lead the charge against this perceived danger to science from both within and outside the academy, and the rhetoric was heated. Philosopher

Mario Bunge said, "Walk a few steps away from the faculties of science, engineering, and medicine. Walk towards the faculty of arts. Here, you will meet another world, one where falsities and lies are manufactured in industrial quantities. . . . We should expel these charlatans from the university." "The sole remedy at our disposal," according to philosopher Barry Gross, "is to quarantine the anti-science brigades and inoculate the rest of the population against them. Scientists will have to devote some of their energy to systematic confrontation with the enemies of science" (Hoke 1995).

But the very vehemence of this counter-attack may be backfiring on science. Rather than coming across as reasonable defenders of the scientific worldview, these scientists risk being perceived as arrogant elitists who sneer at those who do not understand them and adopt a scorched-earth policy against those who disagree with them.

At present there seems to be very little attempt by any of the protagonists in the science-religion wars to really understand what the other groups are saying. The debate often is cast in apocalyptic terms with each side determined to "win" the hearts and minds of the general public and forecasting dire consequences if they "lose." In the view of elite science, a "win" for fringe beliefs will be the end of civilization as we know it, with rampant ignorance and superstition eventually driving out science from decision making, giving respectability to astrologers and other charlatans, and replacing reason with gullibility and foolishness. In the view of creationists, if they "lose" this also will be the end of civilization as we know it, the first step in the march toward rampant atheism, moral degeneracy, and, of course, secular humanism.

Given that this is ostensibly a battle for public acceptance of their worldviews, the vitriolic tactics that have been adopted by both sides seem more likely to alienate people than to win them over. Rather than being convinced by one or the other side, the public is more likely to wish a pox on both houses and tune out the debate. That would be a pity because the issues raised are deeply interesting and have profound implications for anyone who seeks an understanding and synthesis of science, religion, and philosophy. The purpose of this book is to provide a framework to take a fresh look at this problem.

Searching for Truth

If, as suggested above, the soothing middle ground that "religion and science are separate and mutually exclusive realms of human thought" is untenable, then it does seem as if we are left in the position of having to choose between two irreconcilable propositions: either the naturalist view (all phenomena follow natural laws without exception) is correct or the creationist view (life as we know it could not have come about without at least occasional divine direct intervention) is correct. How does one go about making such a choice? In order to do so, there needs to be a consensus on what constitutes the facts to be interpreted, what exactly are those things we call theories, what rules and judgments constitute a validation or refutation (or falsification) of a theory, what exactly constitutes "science," whether naturalism and creationism are the only viable competing models so that refutation of one implies the acceptance of the other, and so forth.

This debate involves the search for "truth." It has long been realized that truth is a subtle and elusive concept, especially in the world of ideas. Pontius Pilate's sardonic query, "What is truth?" — revealingly added to in the rock musical *Jesus Christ Superstar* with, "Is mine the same as yours?" — illustrates the ambiguity and subjectivity associated with this concept. But when we are dealing with *scientific* knowledge, this ambiguity is popularly believed to not exist. Science is believed to be the one area where objective judgments can be made about competing theories. Surely, then, we should be able to determine whether naturalism or creationism is true (or at least if either one is false) because they both claim to be scientific explanations of the world around us. If so, then why have we still not been able to do so? Is it because (as each side asserts) the other side is being willfully obtuse and dogmatic in refusing to yield to the evidence?

Returning to the main argument of creationists, the basic assumption that lies behind the superweak creationist position (Johnson 1991) is that there are two, and only two, possible explanations for the evolution of life — creationism and evolution — and that either one or the other, *but not both*, must be correct. This leads the superweak creationists to feel they need not advance any arguments in favor of the creationist position. Instead, they adopt the strategy of focusing their energies on finding flaws in the case for evolution, believing that any argument against evolution is automatically one in favor of creationism. If the arguments against evolution are serious enough to warrant skepticism of evolution, then creationism wins by default. This is the crux of the superweak creationist position. Later on in this book I will examine this assumption and find it wanting, thus undermining the effectiveness of the entire strategy.

In Part I of this book I look at the role of truth in the development of knowledge and conclude that this concept cannot be used to evaluate the relative merits of differing theories or worldviews. This conclusion will be profoundly disturbing to those who like to believe that there exists a hierarchy of knowledge in which beliefs that are considered "respectable" (such as those of science or mainstream religions) occupy the apex while those of "dubious" repute (usually labeled pseudo-science or even quackery) are at the bottom. Such people will fear that denying the role of "truth" in forming judgments will mean that all belief structures will have to be considered equally true (or false) and that this will result in the proliferation of all kinds of crackpot theories.

In Part II of this book I provide some relief to those who find this situation intolerable. I propose an alternative model of knowledge that does allow for discrimination between different belief structures. Although we cannot say that one theory is *truer* than another, it is possible to say whether it is *better.* But to be judged better means answering the question, "better for what purpose?" Thus the value of any form of knowledge is dependent on the *purposes* for which that knowledge is required and the mechanism by which it is created. As long as knowledge is serving a need, it is valid. Scientific knowledge serves a particular kind of need and is created by one mechanism. Religious knowledge serves a different need and is created by a different mechanism. But this position will not satisfy those who view it as another kind of relativism and who yearn for an absolute standard that can be used to adjudicate between alternative belief structures.

There remains one important, subtle, implicit, and difficult issue to be addressed, and that is the relationship of each of these knowledge structures to reality. The reason for the importance of this point is that it seems to avoid the slippery slope of relativism. If there is a unique external (objective) reality that exists independently of us, then shouldn't we be able to compare each form of knowledge with this unique reality and determine which of the two belief structures (naturalist or creationist) provides us with the most accurate representation of that reality?

In order to appreciate and answer this question, we will have to go well beyond the question of creationism versus naturalism and create a generalized theory of knowledge. We will have to address such questions as: What exactly is knowledge? How do we acquire it? How do we judge its validity? How do we decide between two competing models of knowledge? What is the nature of reality?

The search for answers will take us far beyond the questions posed in this introduction, but I will return to them in Part III. The solution to the science-religion conflict that is proposed in this essay is unlikely to appeal to everyone, given the sensitive and controversial nature of the topics involved. It will give cold comfort to those who, albeit with the worthy goal of supporting rationality, wish to stamp out fringe belief structures completely. But I hope that all readers will be left at least with a deeper understanding of the issues and have a framework in which those issues can be discussed without animosity.

PART I

CHAPTER ONE

THE NATURE
OF KNOWLEDGE

The difficulty lies not in new ideas but in escaping from old ones.

— John Maynard Keynes

Next to breathing, learning is probably one of the most unconscious acts that human beings perform. Learning goes hand in hand with living, creating in each individual a storehouse of knowledge that can be drawn on as needed. But what is going on when we learn something? What exactly is knowledge and how is it related to the world that we live in? Are science, religion, history, and so forth, different kinds of knowledge? Do they each tell us something about different aspects of the same reality or are they windows into different worlds altogether? If, for example, scientific knowledge is different from other forms of knowledge, in what ways does it differ?

These questions are central to the ideas developed in this book. In order to start the process of exploration into these questions, let us take a simple model of knowledge that is widely accepted. There is an external world, which we call reality, that exists independently of us and irrespective of our view of it. Although we, as individuals, are part of the world and can influence it and are influenced by it, this effect is minimal and can be ignored. This external world that exists independently of us is thus referred to as an *objective* reality, to be contrasted with a *subjective* reality that exists only in our own minds and will disappear along with us. Knowledge is the information that describes the world; and if the world has an objective reality, then this information also must exist independent of us. It is this knowledge that frequently is referred to as "the truth." Science is the means by which we gain the most reliable knowledge about this independently existing world. As scientific knowledge develops to provide us with an increasingly accurate and comprehensive description of reality, we approach "the truth."

Is this simple model correct? Can we prove these assertions? Or are they simply articles of faith that we have grown accustomed to but cannot justify? To many people, the above statements seem so self-evident that it will be considered a waste of time even to raise these questions. But the statements are not self-evident. This chapter will seek to examine all of these issues in some detail and to apply to them the methods of scientific analysis that we use with all other forms of knowledge. This exploration will take us down paths that some may find surprising and even disturbing because it suggests that what we call "reality," and the relationship of knowledge to that reality, are both somewhat different from what is commonly assumed.

Let us start with what seems to be an easy question: Is knowledge increasing? The answer to this seems so obvious that even to ask it invites ridicule. We are, after all, supposed to be living in an information age. Experts tell us that knowledge is growing at an exponential rate so that the sum total of human knowledge is doubling every few years. The current generation of students will learn things that would have been inconceivable to their grandparents.

Does this mean that as a society we are becoming more knowledgeable? I think that there would be a general consensus that we are, but the implications of this for our future well-being are not that clear. Some might argue that the quality of the information that is being generated is highly variable and not always beneficial. One also might argue that while society as a whole is becoming more knowledgeable, the sheer volume of information that is becoming available and its increased fragmentation and specialization are making it more inaccessible to individual people, making them more confused and uncertain, unable to find their way in uncharted territory. In this book, I accept without argument the statement that knowledge is rapidly increasing and I am not interested in making value judgments on the quality of knowledge that is being created.

Suppose I offer a related but different question: Is our ignorance decreasing? At first glance, this seems to be merely an alternative, but equivalent, form of "Is our knowledge increasing?" But when asked, people are more hesitant in answering, less sure of the response. Initially it seems intuitively obvious that if knowledge is increasing, ignorance must be decreasing. However, a little reflection will show that the questions are effectively identical only if we assume that the total of knowledge (both actually attained to date and potentially attainable in the future) is a fixed and finite quantity. But is this assumption self-evident? Or is knowledge a different kind of entity that has no limit, so that increasing knowledge does not automatically imply decreasing ignorance? To arrive at an answer to the question about ignorance requires us to examine our beliefs about what constitutes knowledge. In other words, we need to construct a model of knowledge and how it is created and acquired.

I am talking about the collective knowledge and ignorance of society as a whole, not about an individual's perception of his or her own ignorance. It is quite possible that even though people today may know much more than their great-grandparents, they may *feel* more ignorant because they are unable to keep pace with knowledge growth.

What exactly is knowledge? What does it mean when we say "I know" something? This book will approach these questions by first examining how scientific knowledge differs from other forms of knowledge. An awareness of this divergence and its possible unfortunate consequences was highlighted nearly four decades ago by C.P. Snow in his Rede lectures, titled *The Two Cultures* (1964). Snow warned about the danger arising from the sciences and the humanities growing isolated from one another, each one increasingly unable to comprehend the language and ideas expressed by the other. Despite his warning, the situation not only has *not* improved, it is worse. It is undoubtedly true that for the general public science is seen as an important but difficult and esoteric subject that can be understood only by a few people, and then only after many years of full-time study.

The popular media report on scientific matters frequently, but their coverage tends to be superficial and features only breathless reporting of the latest discoveries from research laboratories. This type of reporting enhances the mystique of science at the expense of an increased understanding of the nature of scientific inquiry. Rather than increasing public understanding of science and its underlying philosophy, such coverage tends to intimidate the public even further, giving them the impression that new scientific knowledge can be created only by experts.

We have reached a stage where to be ignorant of science is seen as the *normal* state of affairs and not a sign of a woefully inadequate education, even for otherwise highly educated people. Few people would be proud of being ignorant of art or language or literature or history or music to the same extent they are willing to admit ignorance of science. Scientific knowledge is perceived to be different from the general body of knowledge, and scientists are considered to be (and sometimes are resented as) a new type of priesthood, priests who alone understand the secrets of the universe and on whom the rest of the population must depend to reveal these secrets to them.

What causes this split? Is scientific knowledge fundamentally different from other forms of knowledge; and if so, how? Some features come to mind immediately. Of all kinds of knowledge, scientific knowledge is perhaps considered to be the most objective, in that it is believed to exist independent of human beings. While knowledge in many other areas (such as art, music, law, or economics) is considered to be the creation of humans, science is believed to be saying something about the external world; thus this knowledge is thought to exist even if human beings had never appeared in the universe. One logical consequence of this belief is that it makes it more likely that scientific knowledge is finite when compared with knowledge in any other discipline. If knowledge is something that is created by acts of human imagination, then potentially there is no limit to its extent. But if knowledge is simply a revelation of what already exists (what often is referred to within the scientific community as an objective reality), then it can be finite.

Another key difference is that while knowledge in all other areas *accumulates* (in that new knowledge is added to the old but does not necessarily replace it), scientific knowledge *progresses* in that new knowledge is considered to be *better* than the old and supersedes it. Old scientific knowledge is of little value and usually is forgotten rapidly unless it has some historical significance in illustrating how the current knowledge came about. Few people today, for example, have even heard of the phlogiston theory of combustion even though, until relatively recently, this was the universal view of combustion.

But there is one difference between scientific and non-scientific knowledge that overshadows all the rest. Put simply: Science works. Unlike any other form of knowledge, science provides a means of constructing machines and theories that are unequaled in their ability to predict and to provide control. The whole structure of modern technological society is a monument to the success of science. Astronauts go into space, diseases are conquered, and daily living is revolutionized, all using the precision and technology that modern science has enabled. Any theory of knowledge must explain this phenomenal record. No other branch of knowledge can match it in this regard.

Yet the success of science is not manifested purely in technological terms. After all, many of the great technological innovations of the past were empirically based, predated the important scientific developments in that area, and often provided the impetus for those scientific developments. Science also works in that it has created an intricate structure of knowledge that explains a wide spectrum of phenomena in a reasonably coherent and consistent manner.

I will argue that while the success of science is incontrovertible, it is this very same success that may be obscuring us to the subtleties of science's knowledge structure, leading us to construct a model of scientific knowledge that makes it seem more different from other forms of knowledge than is actually the case.

The words *reality* and *objective reality* occur frequently in any discussion involving knowledge and science. It should be emphasized that objective reality is not the same as reality. The latter usually is contrasted with "delusion," and someone who abandons reality is presumed to be delusional, living in a private world not shared by others. Objective reality is a much less sweeping concept and, as discussed earlier in this chapter, pertains to the relationship between the observer and the observed. It is possible to believe simultaneously that everyone shares a common reality (in other words, we all can agree on what the world is like) while rejecting the notion of an objective reality.

Reality carries with it an extensive history and scholarship as to its meaning, and an analysis of its full philosophical implications is well beyond the scope of this book. I will use *reality* in its intuitive meaning: something that exists apart from us and is not a creation of our imagination. The Earth and its inhabitants, for example, are part of that reality. Objective reality has a more technical meaning and refers to something that exists *prior* to our knowledge of its existence. Most people treat *reality* and *objective reality* synonymously because it seems reasonable to assume that what exists should not depend on our awareness of whether it exists. In other words, *all reality is assumed to be objective reality.* But maintaining the distinction between the two terms is useful and will become essential later, when we look closely at what scientific theories say about objective reality.

Perhaps an example will clarify this distinction. By *reality* I mean the commonly used sense of the word. I exist, you (the reader) exist, and, say, the city of Cleveland exists. We can agree to meet in Cleveland at a certain place and time and go there confident that the place will be there. Things seem to have an existence (reality) independent of one another, and we can all agree on their existence. In other words, we have a common, shared reality. There is nothing controversial about this and most people take it for granted. But most people also assume that Cleveland existed *prior* to our realization that Cleveland exists. In other words, when you first learned of the existence of the city of Cleveland (say, at age five), you did not doubt that the city existed before you were aware of it. This is what is referred to as *objective reality* — that something exists and has existed prior to anybody's awareness of its existence. But did the object exist prior to the *very first* awareness by anybody of its existence? Was Cleveland there before anyone knew it was there? For something like a city, this is a silly question. It makes no sense to ask about the very first awareness, because the city itself is a human construction.

But what about the existence of something that may not be a human construction, something that we are sure no one knows about yet but that we can measure if we want to? The position of a particular electron in a particular atom is an example of such a thing. If I do an experiment and measure the electron's position, I will be the first to *know* where the electron is. But was the electron at that measured position *before* I made the measurement (in other words, the electron has an objective reality and the measurement simply *revealed* to me what already existed), or did it have no position at all prior to the measurement but only obtained one as a result of the measurement? The latter view implies that there is no objective reality and therefore the electron's position was *created* by me and my measuring apparatus.

It should be emphasized that there is no problem about the position of the electron after the measurement. The electron has the measured position and it has "reality." The point at issue is about the electron's position before the measurement. If the electron had that position prior to the measurement, then all reality is also objective reality, so that there is no useful distinction between the two terms. If the electron's position was created by the measurement and did not exist prior to the measurement, then objective reality does not exist, though reality still exists.

Most people implicitly believe in an objective reality because it seems to be such a commonsense view. But can this belief be scientifically justified?

Now what has this seemingly esoteric discussion about objective reality got to do with conflict between naturalism and creationism? Simply this: If an objective reality exists, then there exists a *unique* reality out there ("the truth") that is waiting to be revealed. Science and religion are both attempts at understanding this same reality; and if they disagree, then one or the other must be wrong. Increased conflict between the two beliefs is inevitable as advances in knowledge in each one leaves less room to maneuver for the other. This is what we are seeing now in increasingly harsher tones in the science-religion debate.

The belief in the existence of an objective reality permeates science, at least implicitly, and provides the rationale for most scientific activity. In defining their own role as scientists, the term *objective reality* is used almost synonymously with "the world" and "nature." In the dome of the Great Hall of the National Academy of Sciences in Washington, D.C., are inscribed the words: "To science, pilot of industry, conqueror of disease, multiplier of the harvest, explorer of the universe, revealer of nature's laws, eternal guide to truth." In that single sentence are captured the ideas that science works, its domain of investigation is the universe, there is an objective reality, and scientific knowledge is approaching truth.

Almost any practicing scientist would phrase his or her mission in words that are similar. For example, physicist P.W. Anderson echoes this sentiment when he says, "The basic goal of physics is not mathematical elegance . . . but learning the truth about the world around us" (Anderson 1990, p. 9). It is such a familiar formulation that scientists tend to see its meaning as self-evident. But in this book we will examine that formulation closely and find, I believe, that is not the simple truism it appears to be.

The question, "What is truth?" makes sensible people nervous. It evokes comparisons with such questions as "What is the meaning of life?" and signifies the sort of metaphysical speculations for which there may be no discernible answer and that merely serve as topics for entertaining, but ultimately pointless, discussions among people who like to philosophize. The word *truth* also has different connotations in the worlds of science and non-science. For example, when a work of literature or art is spoken of as saying something true about the human condition, this judgment is perceived as a subjective evaluation, similar to such other criteria as beauty, elegance, style, and technique. The merits of such a judgment, when applied to any particular work of art, usually are not accepted by everyone and often are subject to fierce debate.

But for scientists, the notion of truth is not something related to an individual's perception. It is the principal — perhaps only — criterion that the scientific community uses in evaluating the worthiness of its knowledge. The history of scientific progress is riddled through and through with the notion of truth because the entire scientific enterprise is believed to revolve around the process of trying to find out what is true and identifying and eliminating what is false. So for scientists these concepts are not abstractions or value judgments that are subject to philosophical debate but must have specific operational meanings. It is only then that consensus can be obtained among all members of the scientific community as to what constitutes the best available theory. Scientists need to be clear about what has to be done in order to determine the truth and falsity of all practical aspects of their profession So it is important to examine closely what true and false mean in the scientific context, how scientists decide what is true and what is false, and whether it is even possible to make such a judgment on purely objective grounds.

This immediately raises other questions. Are there any grounds for believing that the methods that the scientific community has chosen to judge the truth of scientific knowledge are, in fact, leading us closer to "the truth"? How dependent is the notion of the truth on a belief in the existence of an objective reality? Does truth even exist in the form believed by scientists?

In this book I attempt to examine all of these questions. It is possible that the answers will disturb many in the scientific community because I will argue that the standard model of scientific knowledge and progress in which most scientists believe has some serious methodological problems and that the history of the scientific enterprise makes more sense if it is viewed not as the search for "the truth" but as a means of increasing our control over the environment — and that one can have the latter without the former.

I propose an alternative model of knowledge that draws together strands of research in modern physics, history and philosophy of science, and theories of learning and education. This alternative model argues that rather than knowledge *revealing* reality, knowledge *creates* it. Furthermore, I will argue that knowledge comes in different varieties to serve different purposes, that it is the method by which knowledge is created that defines its nature. So scientific knowledge differs from other forms of knowledge because the method by which that knowledge is generated is different. This also implies that judgments about which knowledge is "truer" are irrelevant. I also explore the implications of this model for such topics as science education, popular scientific literacy, and the relationship between science and religion.

Although the general purpose of this book is to examine the nature of knowledge in general, much of it focuses on scientific knowledge and physics in particular. It is a peculiar conceit of scientists to think that their own particular discipline alone holds the key to understand the workings of the world. But I have tried not to let that feeling dominate, and indeed there are other good reasons for my choice.

Of the many reasons for choosing to focus on science and physics, one is purely practical. As a scientist, I am more familiar with that world and the kind of knowledge it includes than with other areas and thus am more comfortable discussing it. Within the world of science, my area of specialization is physics.

A second reason for choosing physics is that, since Einstein, physics has been identified in the public mind as a subject that deals with deep scientific truths, profoundly influencing our beliefs about the nature of our physical world. It is popularly considered to be the hardest of the hard sciences, where "hard" refers to its rigor and objectivity (though for many non-physicists the word also describes their reaction to it while in school). Thus their understanding of how knowledge in physics is created strongly influences public perceptions of scientific knowledge.

A more important reason for the focus on physics, however, is that philosophers of science have long considered physics to be a model of good science, and so the evolution of its knowledge structure has been studied extensively.

A final reason for the focus on physics is that, as we shall see later, quantum physics is the one branch of science that directly addresses the specific question of whether an objective reality exists and the relationship of measurements (knowledge) to reality. Thus any discussion of reality must incorporate this branch of knowledge.

There also is a more general reason for my focus on scientific knowledge, which is my belief that scientific knowledge is much more like other forms of knowledge than is popularly thought to be the case. A key element of the argument is to show that the nature of scientific knowledge is somewhat different from what many practicing scientists and non-scientists believe it to be. So while I am concerned about the nature of knowledge in general, my examples will be taken from the world of science and physics in particular. The reader, however, need not know any physics in order to understand the threads of the argument. While specific scientific theories can be difficult for the lay person to comprehend, the overall conceptual framework in which science operates is not hard to understand. It is this latter aspect of science that I discuss in this book.

I have tried to follow Einstein's dictum that, when explaining scientific phenomena, one should "make things as simple as possible, but not simpler." There is a popular and mistaken impression that the physical sciences are difficult because of their mathematical complexity. The real difficulty in understanding science lies in dealing with logical and analytical issues, such as distinguishing between observation and inference, disentangling complex interwoven threads of argument, and, most important, subjecting cherished beliefs and assumptions to critical scrutiny. These difficulties are not unlike those faced in other areas, such dealing with a complex legal case, analyzing the historical and social causes of major events, interpreting the structure of a great novel, or understanding the behavior of individuals. If our educational efforts in schools were better focused, such important skills would be acquired automatically by all students, and science would not seem such a forbidding subject. (I will return to this topic later in the book.) While it is undoubtedly true that mathematics plays an important role in physics research and that it can be intimidating to some, it is a complicating factor and not the prime difficulty — and this book does not require any. So I urge the reader not to shy away from the science questions raised in this book, and I hope that she or he is left with an understanding of how science works and of the rules and limits of scientific inference.

CHAPTER TWO

THE NATURE OF SCIENTIFIC PROGRESS

The philosophy of science is just about as useful to scientists as ornithology is to birds.

— Unknown

What exactly is the nature of scientific knowledge? Is it different in any fundamental way from other forms of knowledge, say, in music or art or politics? In this chapter we will look at one critical way in which scientific knowledge differs from all other forms of knowledge, and that is the way in which the addition of *new* knowledge is related to that which already exists.

In music, for example, styles, instruments, and techniques have changed over the years, allowing for a widening range of compositional forms; and all of the innovations are added on as important pieces of our musical heritage. A contemporary musician has the choice of building on any of the musical styles of the past or inventing a new one. Not all of the genres will be treated equally or command a mass following at any given time. We have had eras of popularity for classical, jazz, swing, blues, rock 'n' roll, rap, and combinations of these forms. Individuals may prefer one style over another and feel that some forms are superior to others; but even those who passionately feel that a particular era was the high point in musical history (be it baroque or rock 'n' roll) will concede that there is no fundamental sense in which one form of music is right and all the others are wrong. Rap music did not replace rock 'n' roll as a better or "truer" form of music. It simply was different and attracted a different audience. Advances in music result in a sort of smorgasbord of accumulated musical knowledge.

This kind of knowledge accumulation is typical of most disciplines. In the case of art, if you are designing and furnishing a building, you can choose from the whole spectrum of possible architectural forms and choose artwork that complements the building structure, the whole process being determined by what you feel is most appropriate for your purposes. Others might disagree with your choice, but there is no single right way of doing it. Similarly, history can be studied using different analytical techniques developed over the years. In politics, a country can choose its form of government from all those that existed at one time or another or can invent a new form. As time goes by, the choices available to the user in all these areas of knowledge keep growing as the knowledge base of the subject increases. Any attempt to assert that one particular form of knowledge is superior to the rest and is the only one worthy of serious consideration would ignite a firestorm of protest from other members of the community.

Scientific knowledge is in sharp contrast to this model of knowledge accumulation. In science, it is accepted by all scientists that the current state of knowledge is superior to anything we had in the past and is the only one that is really worth knowing. The older theories are regarded as valid expressions of knowledge based on experimental observations available at that time. But new evidence is considered to have rendered them obsolete, so that by current standards they are portrayed as either wrong (as in the case of the phlogiston theory of combustion or Aristotle's theory of motion) or as approximations to newer and better theories (as in the case of Newton's second law of motion). Older theories are not always completely discarded. They sometimes play very useful, even essential, roles in our lives. Newton's second law, for example, is still one of the most useful laws in physics because it is relatively easy to understand, requires fairly simple mathematics to implement, and yet gives very precise results for an enormously wide range of phenomena. Technology at the frontiers of human experience (such as putting people into space and bringing them back) as well as more mundane but indispensable aspects of our daily life (such as the automobile) depend on the use of this law. Thus it still properly forms the foundation of any physics education program.

But Newton's laws, despite their unusual longevity and versatility, are in the epistemological scheme of things no longer considered "true" by the scientific community. The laws are perceived as an approximation to the "true" laws of motion developed by Einstein and others. It is immaterial in this context that Einstein's theory is mathematically far more complicated than Newton's, so much so that students are introduced to it in a reasonably comprehensive form only in advanced college courses; and it is used only in highly specialized situations. Even professional scientists, given a situation where both Newton's and Einstein's theories can be used to get a particular result, will prefer the (approximate) Newtonian mechanics over the (correct) Einsteinian mechanics because it is so much easier to obtain results. So scientific judgments about which theory is "true" and which is "false" have little to do with the range of applicability of a theory. Judgments about the correctness of a theory are clearly being determined by other criteria.

Older theories that now are considered plainly wrong or of limited usefulness are usually forgotten, the exceptions being those that serve a pedagogical purpose. This usually takes the form of theories that were accepted as true at one time but that predicted an experimental result that was in marked contrast to what was observed and which can be explained satisfactorily by the current theory. We will return to such events in the next chapter when they are used as the basis of another model to explain how science progresses.

Thus in science, new knowledge tends to be considered better than the old and replaces it in terms of what is considered "true." This is what is meant when we say that, unlike other forms of knowledge, scientific knowledge can be said to progress. But knowledge once created cannot be destroyed, and so scientific knowledge also can be considered to accumulate. But this is of little practical consequence because the older knowledge is omitted from newer textbooks and ceases to be of value to practicing scientists, though it may still have some archival value to the historian of science.

This implicit understanding of the nature of scientific knowledge is illustrated by the way we teach science compared to other subjects. Each generation of students is taught only the *current* state of scientific knowledge and only those theories that are of value to scientists at that time. Outdated theories are ignored, unless they are introduced to provide a quick historical overview or to show why they were inadequate. The goal of science education is to give students only the current or "best" knowledge. In other subjects earlier knowledge is also valued and taught along with the historical context in which it was developed. A student of art, for example, will learn in depth about all the major developments in art history, such as the romantics, the realists, the impressionists, and so forth. A student of literature will definitely not be required to read only books on the current best-seller lists.

No one would dispute the fact that scientific knowledge is consistently increasing in the details of its knowledge and the scope of its coverage. In addition to knowing more and more details about familiar areas of knowledge, whole new areas of study keep coming into being. These range from the esoteric subspecialties known to a few specialists (such as nuclear medicine) to broad areas that are at least superficially familiar to everyone (such as ecology or sociobiology). Unlike some areas of knowledge, such as politics or morals or ethics, there is general consensus that science is progressing, that its knowledge is growing and becoming more complete and useful. Occasionally there may be concern that some of these advances have resulted in the world not being better off now than it was in the past. Developments in areas of nuclear weaponry and genetic engineering have inspired some serious ethical and moral debates and have generated accusations of scientific waywardness; but these charges usually have been deflected as matters involving public policy, rather than being the direct responsibility of scientists. Scientific knowledge, in its purest form, is accepted as ever-advancing, with new discoveries constantly causing older, erroneous ideas to be replaced in our canons of belief.

What is it about scientific knowledge that makes this difference? What causes it to have this distinctive feature that we call progress? Clearly an important part of this difference lies in the fact that the scientific community feels assured that it can judge what is true or false at any given time. But the non-scientific community may not fully appreciate the factors that provide the basis for this confidence. To better understand the nature of scientific knowledge, it may be instructive to see how it is viewed by three different sections of the population: practicing scientists, philosophers of science, and the non-scientific public. We will see that all three groups tend to view scientific knowledge differently, which sometimes leads to crossed channels of communication whenever there is a public debate on anything scientific.

The formal training that a scientist receives in order to be able to practice his or her profession does not include nor require any exposure to the epistemology of science. Usually there is no requirement to take any course in the history or philosophy of science as a separate discipline, because it is believed that all relevant scientific history will be covered as needed during the training the scientist receives while learning the latest theories and their experimental applications. Scientific philosophy and methodology are considered to be best learned by the actual practice of good science and not by any formalized study of it.

This somewhat casual approach to the philosophy of their discipline tends to produce a surprising level of uniformity in the beliefs of members of the scientific community and is perhaps a reflection of how little divergence there is in the beliefs of the practicing scientists who serve as trainers of future scientists. Such uniformity feeds on itself; it reinforces the belief that the resulting philosophy must be correct if everyone believes it. As a consequence of this method of training, if the average scientist is asked to state a scientific philosophy, the answer usually will be some variation on the theme that there is a something "out there" that we call "nature" or "the truth" or "the world" that has an existence independent of the observer (an objective reality). The role of the scientist is to function as an observer (or, more appropriately, a detective) and find out as precisely as possible what the world is like and how it works.

Theories play a central role in constructing the scientific knowledge that issues from this investigative process. While it is asserted that science is an experimental subject, we do not think of scientific knowledge as consisting of only experimental results. We want our knowledge to have explanatory power, and it is the role of scientific theories to provide a context and meaning to experimental results. The scientific observer does this by making measurements of specific features of the world and trying to identify patterns or systematic features from these measurements. The scientist then inductively asserts the existence of a hypothesis that explains the experimental results. If the hypothesis is of general utility and meets with some success, it is sometimes called a theory. Thus theories are acts of human imagination that are arrived at inductively, going from a few, specific, concrete results to a general rule believed to be applicable in all such situations.

To many non-scientists, the words used in science often can be confusing and misleading because they mean different things in science when compared with their everyday usage. Consider the words *hypothesis, theory, law,* and *fact*, which occur repeatedly in any discussion of science. Since language plays an important role in understanding the state of knowledge within science, getting agreement on what these key words mean is important if we are to have a meaningful dialogue between scientists and non-scientists.

Suppose we think of the different kinds of knowledge represented by these words as occupying a hierarchy, ranging from the knowledge we are least confident about to that about which we are most certain. Everyone, scientist and non-scientist alike, will agree that a *hypothesis* is a sort of educated guess and occupies the lowest rung in the hierarchy of knowledge. At the other end of this hierarchy lies a *fact*, which is an experimentally observed and measured quantity and forms the most certain kind of knowledge.

But the words *theory* and *law* are used in very different senses within and outside the scientific community and this influences their positions within the hierarchy. Non-scientists use the word *theory* to signify something that is unproven (close in meaning to the word *hypothesis* but just a little more elaborate), while a *law* is seen as being a theory that has been proven to be true and is thus more like a fact. When used in popular discourse, the word *theory* often is prefaced by the word *mere*, thus emphasizing its lowly status. So for the general public, a law occupies a higher status in the hierarchy of knowledge than a "mere theory."

In fictional crime literature, the stereotypic unimaginative police officer who sneers at the clever amateur detective's hypothesis — "That's a nice theory, but where are the facts?" — reflects the popular understanding of the word *theory*, and this popular understanding is the basis of some of the attacks on the teaching of the theory of evolution in schools. Critics of evolution frequently argue that science is supposed to concern itself only with the teaching of facts and thus should confine itself to exper-imental results and the *laws* of science. They proceed to charge that since scientists themselves refer to the prime mechanism of evolution as the "theory of evolution by natural selection," they are tacitly acknowledging it to be unproven. Hence, these cre-ationists conclude, evolution should either be omitted from the curriculum or be taught on a par with other things that cannot be proven, such as creationism.

But scientists understand the words *theory* and *law* quite dif-ferently than do nonscientists. Both words are used by them to signify theoretical constructs that superimpose a pattern on what would otherwise be unconnected facts. Both words are used to describe fairly sophisticated models that are consistent with a broad range of facts. There is no value judgment made by scien-tists based on these words. Einstein's special theory of relativity is considered to be on far firmer scientific ground than Newton's

laws of motion in the sense that there are no known serious violations of the former (labeled a theory) while the latter (labeled a
law) is known to not work under certain conditions.

Whether something gets called a law or a theory (or sometimes
a "principle") is an accident of history and nothing more, and
they do not occupy different points on the knowledge hierarchy.
A law, just like a theory, is arrived at inductively, based on an
observed pattern of experimental results. Both theories and laws
are understood by scientists to be products of human imagination
and creativity whose goal is to provide coherent and meaningful
explanations of observed phenomena.

Practicing scientists in general would agree that theories are
different from scientific *facts*, which are believed to be incontrovertible experimental observations and measurements made
under rigorous, and usually repeatable, conditions. It is the interplay between theory (or law) and experimental fact that forms the
key to understanding the traditional model of how scientific
knowledge progresses.

Non-scientists are sometimes a little surprised when I tell them
that there exists no scientific body whose role it is to periodically evaluate theories to see if they have passed some test of truth
and can thus be elevated to the status of a law, or to consign a law
into the scientific dustbin if it subsequently fails the test of truth.
It seems incredible to them that scientists attach no special significance to whether something is called a theory or a law.

One useful, though not rigid, distinction that can be (and is)
made between theory and law is to reserve *law* to describe an
inductive generalization suggested by selected observations,
while a *theory* is a conceptual scheme or an explanatory model
used to interpret experimental data. For example, Boyle's law is
a statement that is a generalization based on selected observations
on the pressure and volume of gases, while the kinetic *theory* of
gases is not a single statement at all but is a model that seeks to
explain how Boyle's law, among others, comes about. Thus the
two words can have distinct usages even though they need not
occupy different points on the hypothesis-fact continuum.

Apart from the label issue, the idea that there should be some sort of test to determine if a theory (or law) is true seems perfectly reasonable. After all, if scientists believe that their goal is to seek the truth and if theories are the method by which we interpret the world, then scientists should have a mechanism to judge whether theories are true or not. Otherwise how can we be confident that science is actually progressing, continuously rejecting older false theories while accepting newer true theories? This is why it is so important for the scientific community to have a commonly accepted yardstick for measuring the truth or falsity of theories.

What constitutes a proper test for the truth of a theory is somewhat problematic. It was realized a long time ago by philosophers of science that it was hard to prove that a theory was true in any absolute sense of the word. This is not understood very well by the public (and even by some scientists) and hence it is unsettling to them when the scientific community declares that something once considered true is now false, or at least not known to be true. How can a theory pass a test and be considered true and then subsequently fail? It is a little like a physician who is certified to practice medicine and who later has his or her credentials revoked. People can accept that this can happen occasionally by mistake, but repeated such occurrences would imply that either the certifying bodies were incompetent or that the certification standards were inadequate.

The public often faces these questions when reading media reports. The public frequently is confronted with one reversal after another from the medical science community. For example, media reports that scientists were hailing oat bran as a cancer preventer were followed by reports that downplayed its usefulness, or reports that demonized eggs and cholesterol were followed by more ambivalent reports, and so forth. These reversals can create a sense of cynicism in the public, leading some to believe that scientists' conclusions are not to be treated seriously.

However, scientists tend to be not overly alarmed by these reversals. They understand the limitations under which their colleagues have to work and are willing to concede that new knowledge may reveal that what we now believe to be true is, in fact, wrong or approximate or incomplete. In extreme cases, they may place the blame on the shoulders of those who initially proposed the wrong idea, saying that the full range of evidence was not available to them, and hence they may have overstated their confidence in their conclusions. Scientists remain confident that, while in the short run there may be temporary detours from the path to truth, eventually correct theories will always win out over incorrect ones.

In fact, such reversals are the *norm* and not the exception. There are very few scientific beliefs that have come down the ages intact. Does this mean that our scientific predecessors were less scientific than we are, more prone to errors, less rigorous in applying the test of truth to their scientific theories? This hardly seems likely. While the available technology has undoubtedly advanced, there is no reason to believe that the present generation of scientists is better or more careful than those who came before. Hence understanding the mechanism by which these reversals can occur is an important key to understanding scientific progress.

How do scientists decide if a theory is true? Science education at the precollege and even the college level tends to give a misleading picture of this process. Teaching at these levels tends to follow a fairly standard format, which can be called a confirmatory (or "justificationist") approach to science. First a scientific law (say the law of conservation of energy) is enunciated with its terms carefully explained. It is asserted that this law is applicable in all, or at least a wide array of, situations. Students then are shown demonstrations or do experiments that seem to provide results in agreement with the law. The law then is "confirmed" as true. Thus the teaching of scientific laws is generally deductive, going from the general to the particular; but there is little understanding of how the general rule was constructed. Students are left with the vague impression that the laws were "discovered" in much the same way that fossils are discovered.

There are two problems with this confirmatory model of science. One is purely practical and concerns measurement. When an experiment is done (such as measuring the height of someone using a tape measure), what we obtain are readings given by a pointer on the measuring instrument. However, there always is some uncertainty in a measurement, arising from the imperfections of the measuring instruments themselves and from the lack of perfect control over the conditions of the experiment. Hence the best that we can obtain is a *range* of possible values for each measured quantity, and we cannot know each quantity exactly. This makes it almost impossible to say if two measured quantities are equal. For example, suppose that we have two people who seem to be of the same height. Can we say they are exactly equal? If we measure them with a tape measure and both come out to be 5'8" tall, does that mean they are the same height? Is it not possible that if we measured them more precisely with more sophisticated measuring instruments, there could be very slight differences? However precisely we measure them, there always is the possibility that there exist even tinier differences that our measuring devices cannot detect; and this prevents us from ever definitely concluding that two people have *exactly* the same height.

Confirming the correctness of scientific laws runs into the same kind of difficulty because scientific laws usually are expressed as numerical relationships between different quantities that have to be satisfied exactly. For example, Newton's second law of motion ($F = ma$) says that if you measure the force on an object (symbolized by the letter F), and also its mass (m) and its acceleration (a), then the measured value that you get for force should *exactly* equal the number you get when you multiply its measured value of mass by its measured value of acceleration. But the measurement of each of these three quantities carries a level of uncertainty, and this poses a problem in trying to confirm the truth of the law.

Suppose that students are given the assignment to confirm Newton's law. They measure F, m, and a separately, using different measuring instruments. Suppose that the measuring instrument reading for m is 100, but the instrument has an uncertainty of ± 1; and the measuring instrument reading for a is 50 with an uncertainty of ±2. Thus the best measurement we have for *m* is somewhere in the range between 99 and 101, and similarly the inferred result for *a* is somewhere between 48 and 52. If the students multiply the lowest possible values of *m* and *a* (99 x 48) and then multiply the highest values (101 x 52), they have a possible range of values for *ma* of 4,752 to 5,252. Now suppose that the measurement for *F* is 4,800 with an uncertainty of ±100. The possible values of *F* (4,700 to 4,900) lie, at least partly, within the allowed range of values for *ma*, so there is a possibility of agreement. But we cannot be sure if the relation *F* = *ma* is agreed with *exactly* because we don't know any of the items exactly. All we can say is that the possibility exists that the relationship is satisfied, but it also could be true that it is not satisfied.

Unfortunately, the teaching of science in schools tends to skirt the profoundly important truth embedded in this simple aspect of measurement. Students are given the impression that whatever reading the measuring instrument gives them is the exact value, and they are taught to ignore the uncertainties inherent in the measurement. Thus they expect to find exact agreement for F = ma (after all, this is called a "law" and thus carries with it great prestige). Since the intrinsic uncertainties make this extremely unlikely to happen, some students resort to adjusting their data to fit the theory. Students are taught that their data must agree with the law. They might blame faulty equipment for the disagreement, assume their results are "close enough" (a purely subjective judgment), or surreptitiously adjust one or more result to get exact agreement. Which strategy they adopt usually depends on their perception of the teacher.

This pernicious practice is harmful to science in many ways. It gives students (who constitute the general public of the future) a completely erroneous notion of how science creates knowledge. It breeds skepticism about science because it seems as if scientific laws do not strictly apply to the real world and that experimental data (representing the real world) have to be manipulated in order to conform to the requirements of the theory. And it makes the students feel that they are incompetent and that they should have found an exact agreement if they had done the exper-iment well. This accentuates the feeling that only professional scientists can do science.

There *always* will be an element of uncertainty because each measured quantity is not known precisely but only within some range of values. So while the relationship might be satisfied with-in this range of values, we cannot be sure that it was exactly sat-isfied. It is, after all, conceivable that the numbers would be found *not* to agree if the factors could be measured exactly. It should be emphasized that this is the *normal* situation in science, not the exception, and thus must be addressed when we are talk-ing about scientific progress. If scientific laws are represented by numerical relationships and if we cannot ever determine if the relationships are exactly satisfied, how can we say that an exper-iment confirmed a law to be true?

The second problem with the confirmatory approach is even more serious. A law is not a statement about a relationship involv-ing just *one* particular set of values for the relevant quantities. It is assumed to be valid for *all* the possible experiments that can be carried out within its domain. Newton's law is not about the accel-eration of just one particular mass when one particular force acts on it. It is believed to be true for *all* masses and *all* forces. So even if we ignored the problem of uncertainties and could confirm it for one case, how can we be sure that it is true for all cases? While any non-trivial theory will allow for the prediction of an infinite number of experiments, we can perform only a finite number of all the possible experiments allowed by any theory. How many confirmatory results would be needed before a theory would be accepted as true? How can we arrive at any particular requisite number of experiments that is not purely arbitrary?

As another example, suppose that evolutionary theory predicts the existence of a certain kind of fossil. If such a fossil is found, that supports the theory. But suppose another similar, but slight-ly different, fossil is found nearby. Does the second discovery make the theory 'truer' in some sense? Does it matter if the sec-ond fossil discovery is discovered far away from the first? How does one judge whether new facts are adding significant new knowledge?

The question can be posed more sharply when there are competing theories vying for acceptance. Suppose that in some area of science, one theory explained one set of experimental results while a competing theory explained a second set of results. Suppose further that the two sets of experimental facts had a partial, but not complete, overlap in their results so that there was a common pool of data that both theories agreed with but the remainder were explained by only one or the other theory. How would you judge which theory was the correct one? Is it the one that explained more results? Although this criterion superficially seems more objective (since it involves comparing two numbers), a little reflection will show that it is untenable.

It is relatively easy to do two experiments that differ minutely from each other. In the case of Newton's law we could, if we wished, repeat the experiment an enormous number of times, each with slightly differing masses and slightly differing forces. Should each experiment be counted separately? Or should they be counted as one experiment? How different must two experiments be for them to be considered to be different? In the case of evolution, is the number of fossils that are found important? There is no obvious answer to these questions, and so choosing between competing theories purely on the basis of the number of confirmatory results they produce is not a very satisfactory procedure.

Suppose we reject the idea of using the number of confirmatory results as the critical factor but instead use quality. Suppose we choose the better theory by seeing which one gives better explanations for the more crucial experiments. This approach may seem more reasonable than crudely counting numbers, but its subjective elements are obvious. How do we decide if an experiment is crucial? And how do we decide which results are better? What criteria should we use to make these judgments?

It is possible to sidestep this problem by taking an extreme empirical view and saying that the only things that can be considered to be true are the actual measured quantities or the instrument readings. In this view, true knowledge consists only of experimental facts, and theories have no place in it. In this case, scientific inquiry consists of just the acquisition of facts and does not have much predictive power. However, science works because scientific theories have enormous predictive powers that enable us to control our environment with increasing precision. They are not just a superfluous superstructure that can be dispensed with easily. They are essential for understanding science, and they also are highly useful. As Kurt Lewin said, "There is nothing so practical as a good theory" (Kolb 1984, p. 4).

Scientists use theories to guide them as to which of the many available investigative possibilities are worth pursuing. Theories are an important part in the evolution of scientific knowledge, and to discard them as unimportant is to throw away most of the power of science. While a strictly empirical position might be appealing to some philosophers, this is not a popular position amongst scientists, who set great store in the value of scientific theories and the powerful and useful new knowledge that such theories generate. In addition, even the strict empirical approach has a fatal weakness, which arises from its implicit characterization of experimental results as facts that are independent of theory.

While scientists recognize the methodological limitations, they often use the following argument: It can be plausibly argued that science works regardless of any philosophical problems that may exist. Science is enormously successful in predicting and controlling things and keeps getting better at doing so. It is unlikely that science would be able to do this consistently if the knowledge it creates is false. Hence it must be arriving at knowledge that is true.

This argument, while appealing, suffers from all the drawbacks outlined above. It rests on the assumption that increasing control implies increasing truth.

Clearly scientific knowledge seems to show inexorable progress, except for the occasional and temporary detour. However, a firmer basis is needed for understanding scientific progress.

As we will see in the next chapter, it was the philosopher of science Karl Popper who seemed to provide a way of determining what we mean when we say a theory is true. He provided a mechanism for making an objective choice whenever the scientific community is confronted by competing theories that are vying for acceptance.

CHAPTER THREE

TRUTH AND FALSIFIABILITY

When you have eliminated the impossible, whatever
remains, however improbable, must be the truth.
— Sherlock Holmes in *The Sign of Four,*
Arthur Conan Doyle

In the previous chapter, we discussed what seemed to be two
insurmountable problems to finding a direct proof that any given
theory is true. One is that the uncertainties that are inevitably present in any measurement prevent us from asserting unambiguously
that the theory gives correct predictions. The second is that, even
if we could make such a judgment for a single experiment, how
many of the potentially infinite experiments do we need before we
are convinced? Five? Ten? One hundred? Any particular choice of
number would be arbitrary. Because science values objectivity,
there needs to be some way of making judgments on the value of
scientific theories that removes this element of subjectivity.

Karl Popper seemed to promise a way out of this impasse (Popper 1962). His insight was that while it is impossible to say definitely if an experiment agrees with theory, it is quite possible, and
often easy, to say that it *disagrees*. Recall the examples we discussed in the previous chapter. We cannot prove that two people
have the same height, because there is always the possibility that
there exist minute differences that cannot be detected using our
measuring devices. However, it often is quite simple to show that
they are *not* of the same height, even without any measuring device

such as a tape. A mere glance is sufficient to convince anyone that an infant and an adult have very different length measurements.

The same is true for more sophisticated scientific theories. Earlier we dealt with the problems associated with proving experimentally that Newton's law, $F = ma$, is true when the two values have overlapping, but not matching, ranges. However, if the range of values of F turns out to lie outside the range of ma, we would be in a position to say something very definite. We could unequivocally say that the relationship $F = ma$ is false, even if we do not know each term exactly, because the ranges of allowed values do not overlap.

Focusing on whether a theory can be proved false seems to be a much more straightforward and unambiguous test because, in order to decide if a theory is false, all we need is a *single* experiment that disagrees with the predictions of the theory. Scientific theories are believed to be statements about nature that are not capricious and brook no exceptions. As soon as the existence of even a single experiment that disagrees with a theory is demonstrated conclusively, then that theory is manifestly false and must be rejected.

This approach to testing theories explains much of scientific activity. Scientists do not spend much time conducting experiments to confirm those aspects of theories that already have been examined carefully and found to contain no disagreements. Instead, scientists focus their energies on those areas which are relatively untested and represent the frontiers of the theory. They seek to push the theory to the limits of its predictive power in the belief that it is at the limits where a theory is more likely to break down. If the theory does not fail the tests, then we have benefited by gaining more knowledge about previously unknown applications of it and thus have broadened the range of applicability of the theory.

But we also benefit (and it is usually more exciting) when the theory *fails* a test, because such an event signals the need for a newer and better theory. Improved theories are the main contributors to scientific progress. Thus the failure of a theory is not usually a cause for sorrow in the scientific community (except perhaps for the original proponents of the now-dethroned theory). In fact, the more venerable the theory that is proven false, the more exciting it is because such a change is perceived as signifying a dramatic advance in our understanding of nature. As John Carew Eccles says (Popper 1962), "I can now rejoice even in the falsification of a cherished theory, because even this is a scientific success."

Thus scientists constantly seek areas of research that they feel have the possibility of proving a theory wrong. This explains why, to the mystification of non-scientists, scientists quickly abandon activity in areas that are perceived to be well established and spend their time on research in esoteric areas that seem to have no practical benefits whatsoever. This does not arise from a mere desire for intellectual gratification at all costs or a sense of whimsy or even perverseness. Scientists, like anyone else, want their work to be useful to society, but they believe that major long-term benefits come indirectly, chiefly as a consequence of finding newer and better theories. And in order to stimulate the search for better theories, one has to first show that existing theories are inadequate.

This also explains why scientists will go to extraordinary lengths to create increasingly precise measuring instruments, even at great cost. For the general public, it seems reasonable that once you have reached a useful level of precision in something (say, making ball-bearings), the law of diminishing returns makes any additional benefits prohibitively expensive. But for scientists, the view is quite different. The more precisely you can measure things, the narrower the range of values and the more likely you are to be able to prove something false. Hence scientists will push the limits of precision as far as human ingenuity (and the funding agencies) will permit. One beneficial spin-off to this endeavor is that in striving to create new devices and instruments with greater precision, scientists frequently make technological breakthroughs that have great value in everyday life.

Paradoxically, this focus on trying to prove a theory false also provides a mechanism that enables scientists to make the claim that a theory is true, provided we change our meaning of true from an absolute sense to a provisional one. This is done by saying a theory can be considered true provided that it has not been proven to be false. In other words, as long as that single experiment that disagrees with the theory does not show up, then we can believe that the theory is true even if we have not proven it to be so. Thus at any given time, the only allowed status of a theory is either that of "false" or "not yet proven false." We can, and do, describe a theory as "true," but only in a provisional sense. This is different from the popular understanding of what is meant by "true."

It is worth reiterating this important point. In this approach, a theory can never be proven to be true by any experimental evidence. However, it can be proven false by any single experimental result that disagrees with the predictions of the theory. A provisional verdict of true can be assigned to any theory that has not been proven to be false, but we must be willing to promptly abandon it as soon as a discrepancy occurs. To quote T.H. Huxley, "[T]here is not a single belief that it is not a bounden duty with [scientists] to hold with a light hand and to part with cheerfully, the moment it is really proved to be contrary to any fact, great or small" (1896, p. 469). Huxley realized, however, that the normal human emotions that everyone has might make this easier said than done, and he is alleged to have also said (Hardin 1959, p. 293), "New truths of science begin as heresy, advance to orthodoxy, and end up as superstition."

This version of Popper's formulation (which is referred to as "naive falsificationism") is eagerly seized on by scientists because it seems to overcome the problem of subjective judgments of scientific truths. It provides a single, simple, objective criterion by which to judge the validity of scientific theories. As we shall see in subsequent chapters, Popper and other philosophers later realized that there were some methodological problems with this particular formulation (hence the prefix "naive" in its name) and refined the approach to deal with those problems. But those refinements have not been adopted widely by practicing scientists, perhaps because most practicing scientists like the appealing directness of the naive falsification approach. It seems to validate their instinctive sense that what they are doing is correct and is leading them toward the truth.

Naive falsificationism also resolves the problem of how to avoid subjective judgments when deciding between two or more competing theories. The falsificationist model requires that we should not waste time looking at what or how many experiments each theory agrees with. Instead, we try to find situations in which the competing theories predict *different* results and then do experiments for those particular situations. For the theory that fails to agree with the experiments, the verdict is swift and merciless — that theory must be rejected as being false, even if it agrees with vastly more experimental results than its competitors agree with. This criterion is extraordinarily attractive because it is unambiguous and objective.

This criterion of falsifiability serves many other useful purposes. It is especially attractive to scientists because it provides a framework for understanding their own history and how scientific progress comes about. Such progress is believed to occur by the steady elimination of false theories, thus leading us closer to the true ones. In this view, the early history of science consisted of few concrete experimental results. Consequently, there existed a huge number of potentially true theories because there were so few experimental results that needed explaining. As science evolves, it generates more experimental results that need to be incorporated into existing theories. This results in the elimination of many theories that are falsified because they come into conflict with a particular new result. The more experimental results that need to be explained, the fewer theories that are not falsified. In this epistemology, it is plausible to believe that eventually we will be left, by a process of elimination, with a *single* theory, which will be "the truth." While there may be disagreements about how far we have progressed along this road, there is no disagreement as to where the road leads. It leads inexorably to the truth.

Naive falsificationism is implicitly accepted by many scientists, but it is not appreciated by the general public. The popular image of science is that the purpose of experiments is to confirm theories, not falsify them. This difference explains why the scientific and non-scientific communities have different reactions to the falsification of theories. The general public understands a "true" theory as one that has been proven to be true by scientists. When scientists later show the theory to be false, the public is disturbed by what appears to be a breakdown in the process of science.

Distinguishing Between Science and Non-Science

The criterion of falsifiability has another major benefit in addition to providing a seemingly objective measure of determining what we mean by true. It also seems to provide a means of making a clear distinction between science and non-science. Popper's model of naive falsification is said to have been initially proposed in order to rebut the claim of Marxists that the socialism they proposed was a scientific theory of economic and social development. By this it was implied that the socialist theory was more rigorous than its rivals. Given the prestige that science has in the public mind, to claim that a theory is scientific always enhances its status because it connotes some measure of objectivity and truth. Hence the use of the label is watched closely by the scientific community to make sure that the prestige of science is not invoked on behalf of beliefs that the scientific community itself has not validated.

Marxists argued in favor of their claim to scientific status by saying that their theory was able to provide an explanation for all the major developments in the history of social organization. While reasonable people disagreed about how well Marxism explained the facts of historical development, there was no simple criterion that could be used to convincingly decide whether Marxist theory was true. Indeed, prior to Popper's model, there was no way to even dispute the claim that Marxism was a scientific form of political theory because there were no criteria to judge whether any given theory was worthy of the label scientific, let alone whether it was correct. No clear marker existed which distinguished science from non-science.

But Popper's criterion of falsifiability seemed to resolve that issue. He claimed that a theory can be considered scientific only if it makes concrete predictions that have the potential for falsifying the theory. In other words, the theory should make at least one unambiguous prediction that can be tested by doing an experiment and which, if found to disagree with the prediction, would require the theory to be declared false. For the purposes of classification as scientific, the potentially falsifying experiment need not be immediately feasible. The experiment might require technology and resources that make it highly unlikely to be carried out in the near future. But that is not the issue. The mere existence of a falsifying prediction is the sign that determines if a theory is scientific.

It is worth quoting Popper more fully on this question. He makes seven points:

1. It is easy to obtain confirmations, or verifications, for nearly every theory — if we look for confirmations.

2. Confirmations should count only if they are the result of risky predictions; that is to say, if, unenlightened by the theory in question, we should have expected an event which was incompatible with the theory — an event which would have refuted the theory.

3. Every "good" scientific theory is a prohibition: it forbids certain things to happen. The more a theory forbids, the better it is.

4. A theory which is not refutable by any conceivable event is non-scientific. Irrefutability is not a virtue of a theory (as people often think) but a vice.

5. Every genuine test of a theory is an attempt to falsify it, or refute it. Testability is falsifiability; but there are degrees of falsifiability: some theories are more testable, more exposed to refutation, than others; they take, as it were, greater risks.

6. Confirming evidence should not count except when it is the result of a genuine test of the theory; and this means that it can be presented as a serious but unsuccessful attempt to falsify the theory. . .

7. Some genuinely testable theories, when found to be
false, are still upheld by their admirers — for example by
introducing ad hoc some auxiliary assumption or by reinter-
preting the theory ad hoc in such a way that it escapes refutation. Such a procedure is always possible, but it rescues
the theory from refutation only at the price of destroying, or
at least lowering, its scientific status . . . (Popper 1962, p. 36)

It should be emphasized that the question of whether a theory
is scientific is unrelated to whether it is true. These are two separate issues. As an example, the statement, "The Earth is flat," is a
scientific statement because it can be tested and found to be false
by any experiment that shows that the Earth is not flat. This has,
in fact, been done. But just because we no longer believe the
statement to be true does not mean that the statement itself is not
scientific. Conversely, the statement that "the Earth is round" is
not scientific because the word *round* has no precise, measurable
meaning. The statement cannot be disproved by any experiment
unless the word *round* is defined carefully so that the proposition
can be tested. Non-scientists might find it counterintuitive and
disconcerting that ridiculous statements, such as "the moon is
made of green cheese," are scientific while reasonable ones, such
as "the moon is big," are not. But understanding the distinction
between "scientific" and "true" is essential if scientists and non-
scientists are to speak the same language.

Using this criterion of falsifiability, followers of Popper's
model argued that socialism is not scientific because Marxist theory could explain only the past and not predict the future. When
Marxism did predict the future and the prediction turned out to be
wrong (as in the claim that the first socialist revolution would
occur in such advanced industrial societies as Germany, whereas
it actually took place in relatively backward and feudal Russia),
then Marxists simply gave a new explanation as to why this
occurred. Popper argued that this was not permitted. For a theory
to be considered scientific, the theory has to make at least one firm
prediction. If the prediction turns out to be wrong, then the theory
must be considered incorrect, at least by the standards of science.

The falsifiability criterion is not as harsh as it may first appear. Popper allowed that if a prediction turns out to be wrong, the scientist is allowed to modify the theory to incorporate the troublesome new data, provided this action does not jeopardize agreement with earlier results. In other words, it is allowable to modify the theory so as to get a new and better theory, by which is meant one that explains a larger data set than the discredited one explained.

However, for any given theory, there are limits to the amount of modification that can be allowed. There has to be some central core to the theory, at least one critical prediction that, if found to be false, would negate the very foundation of the theory so that it could not be modified without changing its very nature. Popper's falsificationist model argued that Marxism was not scientific because it had no such core prediction. Marxists seemed unable to predict unambiguously the occurrence of some event that, if it failed to occur the way they predicted, would mean that the theory would have to be declared wrong. It seemed that nothing could occur that could not be accommodated in some way within the framework of the theory and that would shake the belief of the committed Marxist. While they had every right to retain their beliefs, Popper's falsificationist model disqualified them from using the label "scientific" in describing the theory.

Falsifiability Applied to Religion

The falsifiability criterion has another beneficial side-effect, at least as far as scientists are concerned. One of the thorniest issues in the history of science has been the conflict between scientific progress and religious beliefs. The more spectacular events, such as Galileo's treatment by the Catholic Church, are well known; but there have been numerous other instances, mostly involving evolution theory. The potential for conflict between these two belief systems is easy to see.

Religious beliefs, especially those beliefs that involve an activist deity who can alter the progression of events in a non-predictable way, have no place in a system whose ultimate goal is the explanation of all physical phenomena by means of laws that give predictable results. The logical end point of the present model of scientific progress is that eventually science will know everything and thus there will be no room for an activist deity.

Religious believers have long been aware that their belief structure could be squeezed out as scientific knowledge expands to fill all the available room for knowledge. One response has been for some theologians (especially those in the mainstream religious groups) to reject the notion that theirs is a "God of the gaps" whose existence is proved because it explains the things that science cannot. They argue that God transcends the traditional forms of knowledge and occupies some moral or spiritual dimension that is completely separate from the natural world and hence cannot be accessed by scientific knowledge. Other believers have responded with a pantheistic God who is more or less synonymous with the universe and who is revealed through the working of the natural laws. Hence greater understanding of nature leads to a greater understanding and appreciation of God. Both of these religious views implicitly or explicitly reject the notion of an activist deity who alters the course of physical events in unpredictable ways, and thus these views are not "creationist" in the conventional sense of the term.

Other religious believers take a more confrontational approach to science. These groups wish to retain a belief in an activist deity who can alter the course of events that scientific laws predict. In order to deal with the inevitable conflict that this poses with the scientific worldview, they have challenged the ability of science to reveal the truth.

These believers argue that scientific knowledge is fallible (after all, scientists have been wrong, even spectacularly so, in the past) and that scientists are arrogant in their claim that the physical world is all that there is. Such religious believers claim that there is another aspect of nature, which, for want of a better word, we call spiritual. Science cannot address this spiritual aspect and has no tools to examine it, but the spiritual aspect affects the physical world in ways that are impossible for science to predict.

Does such a spiritual world exist? Debating this issue is exhausting and usually is futile, and most practicing scientists would prefer not to be drawn into it. But how can a scientist respond to this important question without giving offense or being perceived as arrogant or dismissive? Many scientists are also religious believers who would like to reconcile the seemingly conflicting scientific and religious belief structures, and thus a satisfying answer to this question is important to them as well.

The criterion of falsifiability provides an option for responding to the religious challenge. When confronted with the thorny question of whether science precludes the existence of God, scientists can respond that they are competent to answer only questions about things that are scientific. Religious beliefs come into the realm of science only if they lead to concrete and unambiguous predictions that can be tested by experiment and, if the test disagrees with the prediction, can be abandoned. Religious beliefs that do not lead to falsifiable predictions are outside the realm of science, however important they may be. People can believe them or not, but they should not involve science in the discussion. This is why scientists argue that religious beliefs have no place in the science curriculum. They assert that it is not a question of whether evolution or creationism is the true theory of life's origins. A necessary criterion for something to be included in a scientific curriculum is that it be scientific and, according to Popper's criterion of falsifiability, religious beliefs simply fail to meet that test.

At this point I'd like to make a distinction between *experiment* and *observation*. An experiment usually connotes an artificial situation in which some variables can be controlled. An experiment usually can be repeated, thus providing a mechanism for checking the consistency of results. Thus experiments are the preferred mechanism for testing theories. But not all scientific theories can be tested by experiments of this sort. Some (such as the Marxist theories of economic and political development) involve too many variables over which the researcher has no control, while others (such as the theory of natural selection for biological evolution or the cosmological big bang theory for the origins of the universe) are explanations of unique historical events that cannot be replicated. How do we determine if these theories are scientific if we cannot do any experiments?

In addition to laboratory experimentation, scientists also have the tools of observation, and observations can be used to make falsifying predictions. The difference is that the predictions are not about events that have yet to occur (as is the case with laboratory experiments that are planned for the future) but about observations of things that already exist but have not been looked for in the past. In cosmology, for example, specific theories of the evolution of the early universe predict values for the present density of matter in the universe or the relative abundance of various elements. We can, with the help of modern technology, measure these quantities and use these observations as a filter for theories.

Similarly, theories of evolution by natural selection predict the past existence of intermediate stages in species development, and these should be reflected in the fossil record. The absence of such fossil data could cast doubt on the theory, though it could be argued that this is because we have not looked in the correct places, rather than that the fossils themselves do not exist. In either case, these observations (or lack of them) can be used to argue that the theories of cosmology and natural selection are scientific because their fates can be determined by predictions of things that should already exist but which we have not observed as yet.

For the purposes of this essay, I will use the term *experiment* to denote both repeatable, controlled, laboratory-type experiments and observations of the type involved in cosmology and natural selection.

Using the criterion of falsifiability to distinguish science from non-science seems easy enough to do in principle, but it runs into serious difficulties when applied to the creationism debate. In the 1982 Arkansas "balanced treatment" case, the federal judge was persuaded by one witness (the philosopher of science Michael Ruse) to conclude that creationism was non-falsifiable and that hence it was outside the realm of science and should not be included in the science curriculum (Numbers 1992). But outside the courtroom, other philosophers of science, such as Larry Laudan (who, like Ruse, were also opposed to teaching creationist beliefs in the classroom) argued that this was a wrong conclusion (Laudan 1996). They asserted that creationism should not be taught because it *had already been falsified.* Clearly any given theory cannot be simultaneously falsified and non-falsifiable, but critics of creationism still come down on both sides of this issue, highlighting the problems associated with applying the criterion of falsifiability to a specific case.

Part of the reason for the disagreement amongst critics of creationism is that they may not be discriminating between the different versions of creationism. Thus Ruse's view might be correct if the version of creationism he calls non-falsifiable consists of the superweak version. That version is impossible to falsify because it does not make any specific claims for its particular version of creationism. Its focus is on finding holes in the theory of evolution. On the other hand, Laudan's position that creationism has already been falsified could be justified if the version of creationism he is referring to is Flood Geology, which makes very specific claims.

Laudan goes even further and argues persuasively that trying to find the demarcation line between science and non-science is an inherently hopeless exercise. Trying to exclude any particular knowledge or belief structure from science classrooms on the basis that it does not fit some arbitrary definition of science is not only wrong-headed, but the strategy can be easily subverted by slight modifications to the offending belief structure, thus bringing it into compliance with the definition while still leaving its philosophical or religious emphasis intact (Laudan 1996).

But even with Flood Geology the situation is not simple. Take the Flood Geologists' major claim that all fossils were created by a global flood that occurred in 3000 BC. It would seem that this is an easy claim to test. Radiocarbon dating of fossil remnants is a well-understood field of science and has been used to identify fossils that are tens and hundreds of thousands of years old. So it would seem (to scientists, at least) that Flood Geology has been convincingly falsified and that its adherents must be rejecting science altogether if they still cling to it. But the Flood Geologists position is more subtle than that. They do not dispute that radiocarbon dating is an important tool in the scientific arsenal. What they question are the assumptions that scientists use in arriving at the dates.

Radiocarbon dating is based on the assumption that there is a fixed proportion of radioactive carbon produced in the environment, and living things ingest it into their systems in the same proportion. This process of ingestion ceases as soon as the organism dies, but the radioactive carbon in the now-dead organism decays at a steady known rate. By measuring the amount of radioactive carbon present in a fossil and comparing it with the proportion present in living things, it can be determined how long the fossil has been dead. What Flood Geologists question is the assumption that radiocarbon was always being produced in the environment at the same rate that it is being produced now. They point out that a key element in their belief is the global flood, which must have deposited a huge amount of water in order to cover the entire Earth. Where was all this water before the flood? They say that it lay in a huge canopy that covered the Earth. In addition to storing the water until the time of the flood, this canopy also shielded the Earth from the rays of the sun; and because sunlight plays an important role in making the environment what it is, it is possible that less radiocarbon was being produced and ingested prior to the flood. That would result in fewer decays being measured in the fossils now, fooling scientists into thinking the fossils are older than they really are.

It is not the purpose of this book to get into the details of the radiocarbon debate on the age of the Earth and its fossils. Instead, I want to focus on three interesting points that are characteristic of all such debates.

The first is that creationists are not blindly anti-science. They use scientific methods to buttress their case.

The second point is that testing a theory requires more than just agreement on what the theory says. It also requires that all sides explicitly agree on how the theory is to be tested, what assumptions should go into the test, and how the results should be interpreted. Such a consensus usually is present within the scientific community but, as the discussion of the age of fossils attests, may not always exist between two very divergent schools of thought.

The final point to be noted is the important role that auxiliary hypotheses (in this case the role of the water canopy) play in any theory. Mainstream scientists might scoff at the water canopy explanation, viewing it as a mere stratagem by some creationists to rescue a shaky theory; and scientists will try to show that the ages given by radiocarbon dating is corroborated by other methods. But as will be seen in the next chapter, auxiliary hypotheses also play an essential role in mainstream science and cannot be written off as just a face-saving device. To eliminate them entirely would bring scientific progress to a halt.

It is important that we be clear about exactly what falsificationism implies. It does not simply consist of the existence of a concrete statement. The statement that the world was created about six thousand years ago is very specific and unambiguous, but by itself it does not constitute a falsifying prediction. This is because it does not specify the conditions under which the statement would be accepted by its followers as false. It becomes a falsifiable statement (and hence scientific) only if believers and non-believers alike agree on how the age of the world is to be determined. If, for example, standard archaeological, anthropological, and radioactive evidence are accepted by all sides as valid indicators of age, then the statement becomes scientific. But if the believers assert that there is no independent means by which to prove the statement false, then the statement about the age of the world ceases to be scientific. If a theory is formulated in such a way that it never can be proven false, then it ceases to be scientific, however concrete it may be in its statements.

It is interesting to note that if we uncritically use Popper's criteria for what makes a theory scientific, Flood Geology must surely rank highly, since it is more restrictive than most theories and gives very specific predictions for many things. There is no ambiguity at all about the claims of Flood Geology. The only problem, and a fatal one at that, is that there is no agreement on how to test its predictions.

Thus it is not as simple as it may first seem to falsify a creationist theory, or any theory for that matter. The situation is not much clearer on the evolution side. Popper himself initially declared that the theory of evolution by natural selection also did not meet the test of falsifiability and thus lay outside science. Although he partially revised this opinion later, these examples illustrate the difficulties inherent in applying the falsifiability criterion to specific cases.

In spite of these practical difficulties, it is not surprising that this specific contribution of the philosophy of science (the falsifiability criterion) is embraced by the scientific community, either explicitly or implicitly. It helps them demarcate the world of science from the world of non-science and avoids the kind of enervating debates on science and religion that distract scientists from their work. It also provides a model that enables scientists to believe that science is progressing by the steady and systematic elimination of false theories, thus approaching the truth. In this worldview, nature is the ultimate objective judge, deciding between good and bad theories. Experiment and observation are acting as surrogates for nature, providing insights into what is allowed and not allowed. The process seems to be eminently objective and, if allowed to proceed unimpeded, will lead us ultimately to the truth. If the story ended at this point, there would be happy endings all around. But as we shall see in the next chapter, it is just the beginning. For what philosophy of science gave the scientific community with one hand (the criterion of naive falsifiability), it took away with the other.

CHAPTER FOUR

THE PROBLEM WITH EXPERIMENTAL OBSERVATIONS

> Sense-data, untheoretical items of observation, simply do not exist.
>
> — Karl Popper

The "naive falsifiability" approach discussed in the previous chapter, however appealing to the scientific community, is untenable. Its success depends on the belief that theories and experiments are two distinct and independent types of knowledge and that one can be used to test the other. Theories are perceived as human constructs that represent our understanding of how nature works, while experimental results are considered to be facts about nature that we can measure and observe. These facts are believed to serve as impartial guides that can, by being compared with the predictions of a theory, substantiate or, more important, falsify a theory. But on closer examination, this seemingly clear distinction between theory and experiment is blurred.

Popper argued that all observations are "theory-laden." What this phrase means is that we cannot totally separate experimental observations from a theoretical framework, because all experimental observations need such a framework in order to be interpreted and to be meaningful. All that an experiment gives us is just a set of readings on some measuring instrument. These readings need an interpretation, and converting them into quantities that have some meaning for the theory being tested necessarily involves using still other theories.

For example, suppose we were to test Ohm's Law for a wire, a common experiment that is done when students are introduced to electricity. This law asserts that for certain types of materials, the current through a wire rises proportionately with the voltage across its ends. Testing this law requires us to measure the values of the current through the wire and the voltage across the ends of the wire. To carry this out we can use ammeters and voltmeters, which have pointers or digital displays that give us numbers. These numbers are the raw material of our data. However, we need a theory of how these meters work in order to interpret the voltmeter numbers as voltages and ammeter numbers as currents. This, in turn, involves the use of theories of electromagnetism and mechanics, at the very least. So currents and voltages are themselves not 'facts' but are theoretical constructs far removed from "sense data," which are those things that we can see, touch, feel, smell, and hear. Even if we had data that we directly received via our senses, say that of sight, we still would need a theory of light and vision to relate the signals our eyes receive with the message that our brain creates.

As another example, take the theory of evolution by natural selection. Suppose that this theory predicts the existence of a certain type of animal occurring at a certain time in the historical record. Suppose also that archaeological work results in such a fossil actually being found. Superficially this looks like a perfect example of comparing a pure discovered fact (in this case, a fossil) with the predictions of a theory. But even a fossil is not a piece of naturally occurring evidence uncontaminated by theory. To have any use at all as evidence for the theory of evolution, the fossil has to be placed in an anthropological context that requires, among many other things, knowing how old it is. But even such a simple task as dating the age of the fossil requires the use of other scientific theories, such as nuclear physics, not to mention the theories that go into all the instrumentation involved. Interpreting fossil data requires using sophisticated theories in order to extract the particular piece of information that is needed for comparing with evolutionary theory. So it could be claimed that evolutionary theory is not being compared with a discovered fact; instead, evolutionary theory is being compared with all the other theories that went into the process of getting information about the fossil.

In other words, we never compare a theory with nature (through its surrogate, the experiment). Instead, we are always comparing one theory with another theory or several theories. Hence our model of nature as an impartial, consistent, and infallible factual judge that can act as the arbiter between competing theories is not correct. The decision on whether a theory is falsified has to be made on other grounds.

This seems to fly in the face of reason. The scientific literature is replete with stories of crucial experiments that overthrew established scientific theories in favor of newer, better, and more comprehensive theories. The great scientific revolutions of the 20th century, such as those involving relativity and quantum mechanics, provide modern examples of this just as Galileo's experiments did in an earlier age. The photoelectric effect, black-body radiation spectrum, and the anomalous behavior of the planet Mercury are well-known examples of supposedly crucial experiments that paved the way for modern physics by coming into conflict with the predictions of classical physics, thus falsifying the classical theories. If nature, through its supposedly surrogate experiments, is not the deciding factor in this process of scientific evolution, then what is? And how can we explain the remarkable success and consistency in maintaining scientific progress?

At this point, scientists and philosophers of science tend to take divergent paths. Scientists argue that, whatever else may be said about it, science works. They claim that science makes predictions that are largely borne out by experiment and, while conceding that the interpretation of experimental results make them theory-laden, the fact that all the current theories seem to give more or less consistent results seems to indicate that there is some underlying truth to the whole enterprise. Indeed, scientists argue that trying to understand exactly *why* science works so well is not essential for scientific progress. The physicist Steven Weinberg approvingly quotes an unnamed source for the remark that "The philosophy of science is just about as useful to scientists as ornithology is to birds."

But philosophers of science, while agreeing with scientists that science works, are more curious about why it works so well, given its seemingly weak epistemological foundations. This is, after all, the reason why their discipline exists. The research they have done on this question sheds fascinating light on the question of how scientific knowledge evolves; what causes the scientific community to embrace, at any given time, one particular theoretical construct at the expense of all others; and how the transition occurs from one theory to another during scientific revolutions. The works of Thomas Kuhn (1970), Imre Lakatos (1978), and Paul Feyerabend (1993) have been very influential. All of them agree that naive falsificationism is untenable because experimental results are theory-laden. Thus they conclude that one is forced to the position that not only are scientific theories not verifiable, they also are not (even in principle) falsifiable, bringing us all the way back to the beginning question of how science progresses at all.

But philosophers of science go even further. They contend that even if, for the sake of argument, we were to concede that experimental results were pure sense-data and not theory-laden, that would solve only part of the problem. Naive falsificationism would become an objective criterion for determining scientific progress but still would not satisfactorily explain the actual *history* of scientific progress. In other words, it would be a good abstract model of progress, but it would be incompatible with the actual history of scientific thought. The reason for this is simple. If we examine the historical record, we find that no theory ever explains or predicts correctly all the data that lie within its domain. There always seem to exist at least some experiments that give results contrary to the predictions of currently accepted theories.

For example, recall the situation prior to the discovery of the planet Neptune. It had been observed at that time that the motion of some known planets, such as Uranus, were not quite consistent with Newton's laws, which was the dominant theory of that period. If a naive falsificationist model of scientific progress was actually in operation, it would have been argued at that time that this anomalous behavior had effectively disproved Newton's laws and thus they should be scrapped. But that is not what happened. Defenders of Newton's laws (which was almost everyone in the scientific community) put down the failures as being due to possible errors in experiments, calculations, or other unknown factors. The discrepancy, though persistent, was classified as merely an anomaly and not as a falsifying event. The anomaly was investigated by a few scientists while the majority continued to confidently use Newton's laws in their own areas of research activity. This continued for many years without any major controversy until the discovery of Neptune explained the anomalous behavior. In fact, the discovery of Neptune in 1846 was itself strongly aided by the belief scientists had that Newton's laws were true because it enabled them to hypothesize that perhaps an unknown planet must be perturbing the motion of the known planets. Aided by this belief, scientists Adams and Leverrier were able to predict where a hitherto unobserved planet would have to be in order to produce the anomalous behavior of Uranus. This told astronomers where to look in the night sky, and Neptune was discovered, thus converting a potentially falsifying event into a tremendous triumph for Newtonian mechanics. It is the existence of such a strong belief in a given theory that gives researchers the confidence that if they work hard at the calculations and observations, they will find the solution to a problem.

Or take another example that is close to the heart of some creationists, the age of the Earth. Until around the mid-18th century, when geology became an established and independent field of study, the question of the age of the Earth was left to the theologians to answer, and Bishop Ussher declared in 1650 that it had been created in 4004 B.C. As a corollary to this date, fossils and sedimentary rocks were believed to have been caused by such catastrophes as the great flood, and the whole concept came to be labeled "Catastrophism." This corresponds to current-day strong ('Flood Geology') and moderate ('Gap' or 'Ruin and Recon-struction') versions of creationism (Numbers 1992). But in the middle of the 18th century an early pioneer in geology, James Hutton, advanced the notion that the Earth's features, rather than being created by one or many catastrophes, were due to the very slow and steady accumulation of changes similar to the ones occurring currently. This new principle (called Uniformitarian-ism) necessarily implied a very old age of the Earth (estimated at more than hundreds of millions of years) and thus immediately sparked conflict with religious beliefs. This new view, aided by the publication in 1830 of the influential *Principles of Geology* by geologist Charles Lyell, gradually replaced Catastrophism among scientists, and theological speculations on the age of the Earth began to be seen as increasingly irrelevant.

While Uniformitarianism was naturally anathema to religious believers, who tried to discredit it and counter its rising influence, its key prediction of a very old Earth was unexpectedly attacked by someone expected to be an ally, the eminent physicist Lord Kelvin (Faure 1986). Over a period of nearly 40 years (ending around 1900), Lord Kelvin used the principles of physics (based on the rates at which the Sun emitted heat and the Earth cooled) to address this question and placed an *upper* limit on the age as somewhere between 20 and 40 million years. While this did not rescue Bishop Ussher's model, it seriously discredited the Uni-formitarianism model; and geologists scrambled, with little suc-cess, to find ways to speed up geological processes in order to accommodate what they perceived as a very young age.

The controversy between physicists and geologists was even-tually resolved around 1900 by the discovery of natural radioac-tivity and the realization that radioactive processes occurring inside the Earth provided a source of heat that had not been accounted for by Lord Kelvin, thus making his estimates of age much lower than they should have been. For the purposes of this essay, though, what is interesting is that from 1850 to 1900, nei-ther the geologists nor the physicists felt that their respective theories had been falsified, though a strict application of the falsification rule might have required this. Both branches of science proceeded to regard this discrepancy as a mere anomaly (though a highly visible and embarrassing one) that eventually would be resolved.

Thus it appears that it is the presence or absence of a competing theory that determines whether a discrepant event is treated as an anomaly or a falsifying event. As long as no satisfactory competing theory exists, discrepant events are treated as anomalies. When one appears, the discrepant event is elevated to the status of a falsifying event.

Philosophers of science argue that all theories at all times have disagreements with experiments that could be classified as falsifying events. When a new theory is first invented, it usually is very specific entity and responds to a specific need that existing theories have not been able to meet. It takes some time and effort on the part of many scientists to flesh out the new theory by applying it in a widening range of applications. When first created, it typically explains only a few experimental results, is yet untested in most areas, and does not agree with some other results. For example, Newton's theory of motion failed to agree with the observed motion of the moon's perigee for nearly 60 years (Kuhn 1970).

If the Popper criterion of falsifiability were strictly followed, then all theories would be rejected as soon as they are proposed. Yet the scientific community holds onto certain theories for considerable lengths of time and then rejects them suddenly in favor of other theories. During each period of stability, the currently prevailing theory has the allegiance of almost all the community within the specialty relevant to the theory. The problem we face is how to explain this evolution of scientific theories in the absence of any objective criteria for verifying or falsifying them.

Thomas Kuhn (1970) introduces a useful category of scientific knowledge called a *paradigm*. This word has been used (and overused) extensively, and its precise meaning has been somewhat obscured. I will use it to mean a general framework for solving problems in a particular area of science. The word *paradigm*, as used here, includes a core theory or set of theories plus a set of shared rules and standards that determine which problems are appropriate to work on for elucidation of the theory, and the criteria for judging the acceptability of proposed solutions to the problems. Most important, a paradigm is accepted by the scientific community as a common basis for activity so that a scientist can work on increasingly esoteric problems, confident that his or her contributions make a valid contribution to scientific knowledge. I will adopt Kuhn's terminology so that scientific activity within an accepted paradigm is called *normal science* while the transition period from one paradigm to another is categorized by a *crisis* for the fading paradigm prior to the *revolution* that replaces it with the new one.

Kuhn argues that scientific progress requires the existence of shared paradigms with shared rules and standards. The shared paradigms produce a set of puzzles or problems that must have solutions, and it is the belief that such solutions exist that motivates scientists to work extremely hard in increasingly esoteric areas to develop the theoretical and experimental tools that will enable them to solve the problems. It is not unlike the determination with which crossword puzzle aficionados attack their daily challenge. Why is it that enthusiasts will devote many hours to finding the letters that fill the squares? Looked at dispassionately, the whole exercise is a waste of time. There usually is no financial reward, they have not created any new knowledge, and the chances are remote of stumbling over some interesting piece of information while doing the puzzle. And yet, completing the puzzles provides such a great deal of satisfaction that people will pore over them for hours at the expense of other, more ostensibly rewarding pursuits. The key to these puzzles' fascination is that the aficionado knows that a solution exists and there is a reasonable chance of finding it. Also, people tend to gravitate toward puzzles that seem to provide both a challenge and a reasonable possibility of success. Enthusiasts veer away from puzzles that they perceive as too easy or too difficult.

The scientific paradigm plays a similar motivating role for scientists. The shared rules provide a means of judging which solutions are acceptable and which are not. Along the way, certain anomalous features may be resistant to solution. If intense effort over an extended period fails to provide a solution to these anomalies, and if the anomaly is considered serious enough by the members of the community, then science enters a period of crisis. During the crisis, alternative theories compete for the allegiance of the community until one emerges as the victor, to become the shared paradigm for the next period of normal science. In other words, theories are never accepted or rejected in isolation, but only in competition with alternative theories.

But what causes the scientific community to switch its allegiance from one theory to another? And how is it that the change becomes so complete that the losing theory either disappears or is marginalized? It is Kuhn's description of the way that this decision-making process occurs within the scientific community that is the main source of controversy, because it seems to introduce a subjective element that is distasteful to scientists. He argues that the transition process is governed by many factors, not the least of which is the relative power and prestige of the various groups claiming allegiance to the competing theories. And once a particular group emerges victorious, it proceeds to exert complete dominance of its viewpoint through the use of textbooks, which are effectively under the control of adherents of whatever paradigm happens to be dominant.

Science textbooks play a critical role in Kuhn's analysis and are one of the key elements that makes scientific progress seem so consistent, unlike other areas of knowledge. Science textbooks are perceived to be the sources of "correct" knowledge and play an important role in the training of future scientists. After every revolution, textbooks are rewritten in a way that seems to imply the rightness and inevitability of the current paradigm. Alternative theories, when mentioned at all, tend to be used to support the current paradigm by being shown in a historical context as having been unable to explain experiments. The most frequent use of an old theory is to use it as the loser in a supposedly critical experiment. The differing predictions of the old theory and the new are presented as a scientific equivalent of a showdown. The experimental results then decisively show that the new theory is the correct one because the prediction of the old differs from the data.

This version of history is usually a reconstruction made after the new theory has gained its status as the ruling paradigm. The critical experiment was usually regarded as just an anomaly (probably one of the many that coexist with any theory) during the time that the old theory was ascendant; but once the paradigm shifted, the status of this anomaly was raised to that of a critical experiment that disproved the old theory. That the new theory explains this previously unexplained result is given as proof of the superiority of the new theory. Conveniently ignored are those anomalies that the *new* theory does not explain. For example, for a long time the anomalous motion of the perihelion of Mercury was viewed as a mere anomaly to Newton's theory. But after the advent of the theory of general relativity and its success in explaining this behavior, this same motion was elevated to the status of a falsifying event for Newtonian physics.

In this model of scientific knowledge, old scientific theories are viewed as mistakes that occurred due to lack of knowledge or imagination or technology. It is not unusual for the old theories to be described in such a way that present-day students marvel that a previous generation of scientists could ever have taken them seriously.

This rewriting of scientific history in textbooks is used to win the allegiance of the next generation of students to the new paradigm. Practitioners of the vanquished paradigm find their sources of students and funding drying up and either have to switch their own allegiance to the new paradigm or have their theory die with them. It is not unlike the situation after a political revolution. History is rewritten from the viewpoint of the victors, showing the rightness of their cause; and selected incidents from the past are highlighted in order to justify the transition.

In Kuhn's view of the evolution of scientific theories, the relative power and prestige of the groups aligned with different theories and the degree of control they exercise over the writing of textbooks play a large role in determining which scientific theory emerges victorious after a revolution. Kuhn, in subsequent writings, is disturbed by people who claim that his arguments imply that the scientific enterprise is fundamentally irrational. Kuhn argues that the scientific community has good reasons for making its paradigm choices, and that the process is rational even if it cannot be defended on wholly objective grounds.

Paul Feyerabend (1993) takes a different and stronger position. He asserts that the scientific enterprise is essentially subjective. He argues that once we concede that all observations are theory-laden, then we have to conclude that the choice being made is always between differing theories and not between theory and experiment. Since there is no completely objective method of deciding which theory is better, we should reject all claims that any given theory is "truer" than any other. Such claims can never be justified and are simply articles of faith, though scientists might like to dress them up as objective inferences drawn from hard data. He argues that we logically are forced to a position of "anything goes" in which science, religion, astrology, witchcraft, superstition, etc., are all on an equal footing because there is no reason to think that one set of beliefs is more true in some objective sense than are the others. Individual people might *prefer* one form of knowledge over all others; but that is based on only personal convictions. Thus scientists should not claim, for example, that scientific knowledge is *superior* to astrology, because there is no objective way to test that assertion.

Feyerabend also argues that the nature of scientific development always unjustifiably gives preference to the *older* theory whenever two theories are equally successful. Anyone who proposes a new theory to explain phenomena already explained by an older theory has a difficult, if not impossible, task in persuading the scientific community that the new theory should be taken seriously as a competitor. Feyerabend argues that it does not matter

which theory came first, the older one always will be given preference. This, he argues, shows how irrational the scientific enterprise
is and how unworthy it is to receive such reverential treatment
from the general public.

Imre Lakatos (1978) is interested in looking at a slightly different question. While he agrees that all observations are theory-
laden and that this makes the transition from one theory to another
subjective, he argues that the reasons the scientific community
does shift from one theory to another are not explained convincingly by just invoking scientific power plays and control over textbooks, as Kuhn suggests. He argues that there are more rational
(though still not objective) reasons for scientific transitions.

In Lakatos' scheme, the contest is not between competing theories and paradigms, but between competing research *programs.*
He characterizes such programs as either *progressive* or *degenerate. A* theory that is part of a progressive program is one that creates a lot of new problems that provide challenges to scientists.
The existence of these many new problems attract scientists to
this program. The degenerate program, on the other hand, is one
in which the supply of problems is either drying up or provides
few challenges to the scientific community. When the community of scientists clearly perceive one of the competing theories as
part of a progressive program, then the community flocks to that
theory, leaving only those with an entrenched commitment to the
other theory to try and salvage it.

Lakatos argues that it is a mistake to talk of theories as if they
were entities that are tested in isolation. He says that each theory
is accompanied by a protective belt of auxiliary hypotheses and
unproblematic background knowledge, which protect a theory
against immediate falsification. For example, if Newton's theory
of gravitation is true, then we should be able to predict the orbits
of all the planets precisely. Hence finding a planet with anomalous behavior should lead to the immediate rejection of Newton's theory. But that is not what happens. Lakatos says this is
because Newton's laws are protected by such auxiliary hypotheses as *"If* we know the masses and locations of all the planets,

and *if* there are no other massive unseen objects in the solar system, and *if* there are no other factors to change the results, and *if* we have done the calculations correctly, then Newton's laws give a specific prediction." In addition, we tacitly assume that the nature of light transmission and the theory of telescopes and the instruments that we use to extract the requisite observational data are part of the unproblematic background knowledge. In other words, it is assumed that we are very confident in the reliability of the theoretical underpinnings of the observations. Note that we cannot *prove* that the auxiliary hypotheses and unproblematic background knowledge are true. It is just an assumption that is made for convenience and which can be revoked when necessary.

Thus when we measure the motion of one of the planets, we are testing the entire package consisting of Newton's laws, the auxiliary hypotheses, and the unproblematic background knowledge. If the measurement happens to disagree with the prediction, it is not apparent where to place the blame. The fault could lie in the core theory (in this case, Newton's laws) or in the auxiliary theories or in the unproblematic background knowledge. Lakatos argues that if the core theory is part of a progressive research program, then its adherents protect the core theory by investigating the validity of the auxiliary hypotheses and the unproblematic background knowledge. Since one always has an inexhaustible supply of possible causes, the core theory can be protected from almost any challenge by postulating other mechanisms to explain the anomaly, thus providing many more puzzles for people to work on. This provides even more normal science activities for scientists and helps build up the body of knowledge surrounding the paradigm.

However, degenerate research programs are not so lucky. When an experimental result comes into conflict with the predictions of the core theory of such a program, the scientific community does not leap to its defense by postulating alternative mechanisms to explain the discrepancy while leaving the core theory intact. Instead, it is assumed that the auxiliary hypotheses are valid and the unproblematic background knowledge is indeed unproblematic, thus leaving the core theory exposed and vulnerable to challenge. This happens when modifications to the auxiliary hypotheses do not provide sufficiently interesting puzzles for scientists.

A good example of how even a simple observation can be theory-laden is the example of what happens when you drop a stone from the top of a tall tower. That the stone fell at the foot of the tower had been used for centuries prior to Galileo to support the belief that the Earth was stationary. It was argued that if the Earth moved, then the stone would hit the ground at a distance from the base of the tower equivalent to the distance moved by the Earth during the time of fall. However, Galileo (by invoking auxiliary hypotheses) used the same phenomenon to support Copernicus' theory that the Earth did move around the Sun (Feyerabend 1993). As Feyerabend argues, the fact that the same sense-data could be used to support two contradictory theories was made possible because Galileo changed the language used to interpret the observation in order to achieve his goal of proving the correctness of Copernicus' views. An observation that once was used to argue against the heliocentric system became an argument in favor of it by changing the auxiliary hypotheses. The incentive to do so was provided when the geocentric system became a degenerate program, incapable of generating new and interesting problems, and thus ripe for discrediting.

Similar transformations can be found in other areas of knowledge in everyday life. In criminal cases involving poor defendants who cannot afford high-powered legal help, official statements from the police, forensic and other experts, laboratories, and other official agencies tend to be regarded as incontrovertible evidence, and the defense has to depend largely on character and alibis in order to protect their core theory (the innocence of the client). But if a defendant has the financial resources to mount a vigorous defense, each aspect of the prosecution's case is open to challenge and is considered vulnerable. All the evidence that usually is considered unproblematic background knowledge suddenly becomes open to scrutiny. This pattern can be observed in any high-profile legal case that has wealthy defendants.

This still leaves the question of how a new theory becomes part of a progressive research program, displacing its predecessor. A new theory typically claims to explain only a few results, since only one or a few people are involved in its creation. Lakatos claims that it increases its appeal and gains adherents if it makes spectacular new predictions that are in agreement with subsequent experiments and if these predictions lead to questions that would not have arisen under the old paradigm. In other words, there is an element of surprise in the nature of the predictions because the new theory addresses questions that were not raised by the old theory. If this happens, then the new theory gains attention and new adherents who can add to its store of successful results, provided the new theory generates plenty of new problems to work on. Thus a new protective belt is created around the new theory.

Lakatos (1978) argues that new theories should be treated gently so they will they have a reasonable chance of generating new results and their own protective belts. However, timing is critical for the success of a new theory; and it is quite possible that many promising avenues of investigation have been unexplored because they happened to come along at the wrong time. If a promising new theory comes along during the heyday of an older theory, the newer theory has little chance of survival because there is no interest in disproving the old theory.

It is difficult for most scientists to accept that all observations are theory-laden. Most scientists are accustomed to thinking of experiments as objective entities independent of any theoretical construct. However, they are aware of the existence of this problem. At professional meetings of physicists, one frequently hears a speaker (usually an experimentalist) mention how a theoretical model originally produced a prediction that was contradicted by a subsequent experiment, whereupon the same theorists discovered that their theory needed some modifications which, when implemented, brought about good agreement with the experimental observations. These remarks are usually greeted with some good-natured laughter at the expense of theorists. Good-natured because everyone realizes that such theory modification (if not perceived as purely ad hoc) is an essential element of scientific progress.

In addition, scientists do implicitly acknowledge the role of theory in extracting meaningful experimental data from the readings on their instruments. In order to sift through the immense amount of data generated by an experiment in order to find that which is of interest for testing a theory, an experimentalist must, by necessity, also be a theorist. And in that process of extraction of meaning, other theories are also involved. Judgments always have to be made about the relative validity of competing theories in any given situation; and, unfortunately, there seems to be no perfectly objective way of making those judgments.

The creationism-naturalism debate provides an almost textbook Kuhnian example of two paradigms that use different criteria for deciding what is true and false. The superweak creationist side starts with the assumption that creationism and evolution by natural selection are the only two viable models for understanding life and the universe. The creationists then point to weaknesses in the theories of evolution and declare that these flaws have effectively falsified that theory. They dismiss evolutionary theory's protective belt of auxiliary hypotheses (such as that the paucity of fossils of intermediate life-forms being due to the extreme difficulty of finding them) as mere excuses designed to hide the fatal flaws of the theory. Since their own creationist theory is protected from falsification by its own protective belt of auxiliary hypotheses, they declare that, by elimination, creationism must be the one true theory.

Their naturalist opponents see things differently, of course. They assert that their own protective belt of auxiliary hypotheses are a valid extension of the scientific method and that hence their theory has not been falsified. Conversely, they argue that the creationists' protective belt (such as that radioactive decay rates are not good predictors of age because they neglect the effect of the water canopy) makes creationism non-falsifiable and thus non-scientific. Each side also challenges the other side's interpretation of the geologic and fossil data.

We see that each side in the creationism-naturalism debate uses different core theories, different protective belts of auxiliary hypotheses, and different criteria for judging their validity. Hence it should hardly be surprising that the conflict has not resolved itself and will never resolve itself as long as the debate continues in its current form. In the next chapter, we will examine the role that scientific reductionism plays in this discussion.

CHAPTER FIVE

SCIENTIFIC REDUCTIONISM

Small is beautiful.

— E.F. Schumacher

Science is split into various subcategories of knowledge: physics, chemistry, biology, ecology, medicine, and so forth. Each of these fields has its own paradigms, journals, research protocols, and standards. There are subcategories within these broad categories; for example, the subcategories of physics include particle, nuclear, condensed matter, astrophysics, and many others. To some extent, these subcategories are distinct. The practitioners within each field usually are unaware of developments in the other areas except in terms that are only slightly deeper than that of the informed lay public.

It is illustrative to look at the ways in which participants in various fields and subfields view one another. These can be broadly categorized into two schemes, one egalitarian, the other hierarchical.

The egalitarian model can be compared to working on a gigantic jigsaw puzzle whose completed picture represents "the truth." Each subfield works on its own section of the puzzle, trying to put the pieces together in a coherent way. All the groups work separately, but they work toward a common goal. Thus, it is hoped, the entire puzzle can be solved. In this model, there is no value judgment made as to which area of science is more important or profound. All knowledge is equally valued, each piece a necessary part of the whole.

Within this framework, the goal of science is two-fold: 1) to develop as much as possible within each discipline or subfield (that is, to complete as well as possible that part of the puzzle each discipline is responsible for), and 2) to solve the boundary problem (that is, to put the various completed sections of the puzzle together to form one big picture).

There is no controversy about the nature of the first task. Each discipline develops its own paradigms, its set of axioms, and its rules of operation that enable it to progress. By continually refining its paradigms in the light of new evidence, scientists within the discipline believe that they are progressing toward a complete description of that part of nature encompassed by their discipline. So far, this essay has been dealing with trying to understand how scientific knowledge progresses as a whole, but the discussion is valid for knowledge within the boundaries of a single discipline or subdiscipline. We have seen that there are problems with the idea that this process necessarily leads us to the truth.

While some scientists might concede that the story of scientific progress is not as simple as falsificationism would have us believe, they would claim that there are other good reasons for preferring one theory over another. These reasons could be aesthetic (the new theory is more elegant) or economic (the new theory is simpler or needs fewer assumptions). However, neither of these reasons is objective. We have no idea if nature demands elegance or simplicity, and to think so is just a theoretical prejudice on our part. Also, simplicity and elegance are themselves subjective qualities, and there may be no consensus on how to apply these criteria in any given situation.

But a third option provides some hope of overcoming the element of subjectivity; that is the model of "scientific reductionism" and the related phenomenon of "theory absorption." Not only does this approach seemingly promise to resolve the question of how different disciplines merge with one another, but it also seems to provide a mechanism for objectively deciding (at least on some occasions) which of two competing theories within a discipline is better.

The process of theory absorption occurs when a new theory is more comprehensive, explains more than the old one, and, most important, incorporates every result of the older theory within its framework. If this occurs, then this can justify the claim that science is moving toward "truth." After all, if the new theory completely encompasses the old in the scope of its coverage so that all the results of the old theory can be claimed for the new, then the new theory can unambiguously be claimed to be superior, since it explains everything that the old one does and more. The new theory can be said to "absorb" the old. In this case there is no doubt as to which theory is better.

This process of theory absorption provides a means of avoiding the problem of subjectivity in theory selection. But while this approach seems to give scientific progress some degree of objectivity, it also results in a moving away from the mosaic, egalitarian model of scientific disciplines and toward a hierarchy of disciplines based on the level of comprehensiveness of the theories they utilize.

The way the hierarchy of disciplines usually occurs within scientific reductionism is in the form of size scales. In this view, levels of knowledge are distinguished by the *size* of the chief constituents that constitute the basis of its explanations of phenomena within its domain. The hierarchy of size scales can be represented on a linear scale, with the social sciences at one end (since its constituents involve the large scale of societies and humans) and, at the other end, physics (which deals with subatomic phenomena). In between are the other disciplines, such as biology (dealing with the structure of living organisms), molecular biology (which has as its constituents such giant molecular chains as genes and proteins), and chemistry (with its constituents comprising molecules and atoms). Of course, these distinctions are not exact, because each discipline contains subdisciplines that can straddle several size scales. For example, sociobiology seeks to explain social phenomena in terms of genetics, while the physics subfields of astrophysics and cosmology deal with the structure of such immense objects as stars, galaxies, and even the universe as a whole.

The reductionist approach proclaims that knowledge within a field lies in knowing two things: 1) the basic components that make up its system, and 2) how they interact. For example, in molecular biology, the search for new knowledge is directed toward identifying all the proteins and other components that constitute living organisms and understanding how they interact with one another to produce the organisms. But the proteins themselves have a substructure, and their molecular and atomic structure form a part of chemistry.

Chemists have as their goal the understanding of atomic properties and how atoms interact to produce the myriad of complex molecules, of which those of interest to biology form only a part. In the reductionist worldview, achieving a complete understanding of chemistry would mean that we also understood biology because we would then know where the components of biology come from and how they interact. Thus one occasionally hears the phrase, "all biology is chemistry."

Similarly, it can be argued that "all chemistry is atomic physics" because the constituent entities in chemistry (molecules) are the subject of study in atomic physics. And the process does not end there. Atomic physics studies the constituents of chemistry, nuclear physics studies the constituents of atomic physics, and particle physics studies the constituents of nuclear physics. Particle physics, almost by definition, deals with the smallest known constituents, which currently are believed to comprise objects known as quarks, leptons, gluons, and other bosons.

Thus each level of knowledge is characterized by its size scale, and this forms a hierarchy of knowledge. The position of each discipline is determined by the size of the constituent objects within that discipline. And the smaller the size scale of the discipline, the closer to truth that discipline is judged to be.

Thus a complete understanding of particle physics would explain how protons, neutrons and other nuclear particles are formed and how they interact to form nuclei. Since these form the constituents of nuclear physics, all of nuclear physics also would be explained. Similarly, once we know how atomic nuclei form and interact with other atomic components, we would have explained atomic physics and chemistry, since we then would know how atoms and molecules form and interact with one another. And once we have completely explained chemistry, then we also will have explained biology, then upward through the ladder to society and the universe. This constitutes the reductionist epistemology.

In this model of knowledge, particle physics theories are the most comprehensive, not because they directly explain all of the phenomena of the other disciplines (the theories of particle physics are of little help in understanding the workings of biological enzymes, for example), but because, by the process of theory absorption, all the results of biology can be claimed for particle physics since ultimately the components of biology can be traced back to subnuclear particles.

This ontological view is held quite strongly by a wide spectrum of scientists and lay people, but especially so (not surprisingly) among physicists. For example, particle physicists dubbed superstring theory, a recent vogue in their field, as the Theory of Everything. Particle physicist Steven Weinberg expresses this reductionist view when he poses such questions as "What is it then about the discovery of DNA that was fundamental to biology? And what is it about particle physics that is fundamental to *everything*" (1987, emphasis added).

Weinberg uses an "arrows of explanation" metaphor in which the explanation of any given phenomenon is given in terms of more basic entities. He asserts that when one understands the workings of the entities that are involved in a phenomenon, then one has, at least in principle, understood that phenomenon. He illustrates this by using arrows starting from the phenomenon and pointing to its constituent entities. There are then more arrows leading from these entities to the yet smaller entities that constitute them, and so on.

This line of reasoning inevitably leads Weinberg to a pre-ordained conclusion: "I have remarked that the arrows of explanation seem to converge to a common source, and in our work on elementary particle physics we think we are approaching that source. There is one clue in today's elementary particle physics that we are not only at the deepest level we can get right now, but we are at a level which is in fact in absolute terms quite deep, perhaps close to the *final source*" (emphasis added). The clue he refers to is that "the rules we have discovered become increasingly coherent and universal," though he admits that the number of constituent particles involved does not decrease and the mathematics required to understand their behavior gets considerably more complicated. It is only someone with an unshakable belief in the reductionist metaphor that can make such optimistic statements. Weinberg subsequently wrote a book, *Dreams of a Final Theory* (1994), whose title illustrates the point being made here.

Weinberg is not alone in his belief. Other particle physicists echo the theme, two of them going so far as to invoke the name "the God particle" (Lederman and Teresi 1993) to characterize a hitherto yet undiscovered particle that is believed to be crucial to an understanding of one important aspect of current theories of particle physics. Finding such a particle, it is believed, would result in us knowing almost everything, hence the name.

It is illustrative that knowledge in every other field proceeds steadily and independently, with their practitioners unconcerned as to whether this "God particle" is found. This particle has no practical consequence for any field other than particle physics. But, in the reductionist epistemology, that is not the point. Understanding particle physics means understanding everything, in principle if not in practice.

This reductionist model of science is very appealing. It frequently is invoked in everyday life when people blame society's ills on the breakdown in family structures, explain family structures in terms of individual psychologies, and so forth. But in practice this reductionist program is not at all easy to carry out. Understanding individual psychology is not sufficient for us to understand family dynamics, and understanding family dynamics is of limited utility in explaining the behavior of societies or the relationships among nations. Despite the abstract, intellectual appeal of the reductionist model, we always need to invoke new concepts to explain things whenever we move to a different area of knowledge. For example, understanding international relations may require new concepts of power utilization and distribution that have little to do with understanding the power relationships among individuals in families and local communities.

It may be argued that the social sciences do not provide a good example because knowledge in the social sciences is very inexact at all levels, thus we cannot expect knowledge on a small size scale to explain phenomena on the large one. But the problem persists even when we apply the reductionist method to situations that seem, at least on the surface, to be ideally suited to the model of theory absorption. To illustrate the difficulty, consider a process of theory absorption that is almost prototypical. It occurs within physics between two theories that are very close to each other and which the physics community itself views as a perfect example of theory absorption. The most familiar and clear-cut examples of theory absorption are the transitions from Newton-ian dynamics to Einsteinian dynamics and from Newton's theory of gravitation to Einstein's theory of general relativity.

In physics folklore, the theory of relativity is portrayed as the correct one, and Newton's theory is considered an approximation to it that is valid only when you are dealing with objects that are moving slowly when compared with the speed of light. This is shown by taking the results of relativity theory and proving that when the velocities of motion are small, all the results of New-ton's laws are obtained. Thus all the results of Newtonian dynam-ics can be claimed for the theory of relativity. It then is asserted that the two theories are not competing theories vying for accept-ance but, instead, one of them (Newton's) is an approximation to, and a special case of, the more complete (and hence better) theo-ry of relativity proposed by Einstein.

From this perspective, the scientific revolution that replaced Newton's theory with Einstein's as the dominant paradigm did not replace an incorrect theory with a correct one. Instead it expanded a limited theory (Newton's) with a more comprehensive one (Einstein's). Scientists argue that Newton's theory is not wrong but only that he and his followers erred in claiming a broader range of applicability than was warranted by the array of evidence available to them. Therefore Einstein's and Newton's theories should not be considered as *competing* theories explaining different sets of data, with all the attendant subjective complications that are involved in deciding which theory should be the victor.

Kuhn (1970) argues that this argument is invalid for two reasons. One is that the very nature of a theory means that it claims to explain more than the things to which it has already been applied. No theory is simply an explanation of things that have already have been measured. Theories have value because they provide insight into the behavior of things that have not yet been examined, thus providing avenues for further exploration. In the absence of any counter-evidence, it was logical and justifiable for adherents of Newton's theory to think that the theory also applied to objects that were moving at any speed.

Kuhn goes on to challenge the notion that Newtonian dynamics can be derived from Einstein's relativistic dynamics as a special case. He argues that to obtain Newton's theory as an approximation to Einstein's, it is not sufficient simply to make the velocities small when compared to that of light. We also have to "Simultaneously. . . alter the fundamental structural elements of which the universe to which they apply is composed. This need to change the meaning of established and familiar concepts is central to the revolutionary impact of Einstein's theory." For example, *mass* has a different meaning in Newton's theory than it does in Einstein's. In Newton's theory mass is a conserved quantity, in Einstein's it can change unless one redefines the term. In other words, going from one theory to another does not involve simply taking the mathematically limiting case of small velocities. It involves changing the language of interpretation of the theory as well. Kuhn argues that going from Newton's to Einstein's theory is as much a revolution involving incompatible theories as was going from the phlogiston to oxygen theory of combustion. The transition is just more subtle because no new objects or concepts needed to be created for the new theory of relativity, just a reinterpretation of the existing language. Kuhn further states that "Though an out-of-date theory can always be viewed as a special case of its up-to-date successor, it must be transformed for the purpose. And the transformation is one that can be undertaken only with the advantages of hindsight, the explicit guidance of the more recent theory."

According to Kuhn, when a crisis arose that forced scientists to choose between Newton's and Einstein's theories, they were not simply absorbing a limited theory into a more comprehensive one. In fact, they were choosing between two incompatible theories. The claim of simple absorption is a later rationalization given by scientists in order to give the final choice an appearance of objectivity and progress. It also enabled scientists to preserve some respectability for a very valuable theory (Newton's) by asserting that it is not wrong, but merely limited in its scope. In actual practice, the paradigm choice made here was not fundamentally different from any other paradigm choice between any two incompatible competing theories and thus carries with it all the difficulties discussed earlier about how to choose the better of two competing theories.

Scientists have ambivalent views about reductionism as a philosophy. Unless examined very closely, reductionism has a plausibility and reasonableness that seem incontestable. Thus almost all scientists tend to find reductionism at least minimally acceptable. But actual enthusiasm for this philosophy varies depending on where one stands in the resulting hierarchy. Many non-physicists have been uncomfortable with scientific reductionism because of its implicit premise that smaller is somehow better. After all, the explanations only go in one direction. Physics can hope to explain chemistry, and chemistry can hope to explain biology; but biology can never explain chemistry, nor can chemistry ever explain physics.

It should be noted that I have categorized the hierarchy among the disciplines purely by their size scales and tried not to relate these scales to the word *fundamental*. The use of that word immediately raises hackles among those scientists (such as biologists) who are in disciplines involving relatively large scales, because it seems to imply that physics is somehow more fundamental than chemistry, which in turn is more fundamental than biology, and so on. And while "more fundamental" should be interpreted as meaning that it is closer to a basic set of axioms of knowledge, its meaning invariably gets extended to mean "more profound." Thus the word *fundamental* often is perceived not as a bland statement about sizes but as a Trojan horse that can be used to set research priorities by determining which area of research is more important.

While uneasy about where the reductionist ontology might lead, non-physicists tend not to challenge scientific reductionism in principle. However, scientists in areas other than particle physics are opposed to what is called "explanatory reductionism," which is the belief that complete knowledge of the properties of the ultimate constituents of matter would be sufficient to explain a more complex system built up from these constituents. This opposition is based on purely practical grounds. The extremely large number of constituents that constitute any but the most simple systems would guarantee that any description based on those constituents would have no value because it would have no *explanatory power*. For example, while particle physics can explain what the components of nuclei are made of, it has little success explaining the nature of the forces between nuclei, except in very vague qualitative terms. But exact knowledge of such forces is crucial to understanding nuclear physics. Similar problems recur as we go up the size scales. The forces between atoms, for example, cannot be exactly explained by nuclear physics, and neither can the forces between molecules be exactly explained by atomic physics. As we go up the size ladder, new concepts and paradigms need to be invoked in order to understand phenomena at each level.

An anecdote told about Einstein illustrates this argument. According to the anecdote, Einstein was asked whether he believed that eventually the entire fifth symphony of Beethoven could be described by mathematical equations. His reply was, "Yes, but it would not make any sense." In other words, even if it were possible to explain biology by using only the concepts developed in chemistry, the resulting explanations would be so convoluted that they would not have any explanatory value, which is the whole point of a theory.

I am not arguing that reductionism is not useful. On the contrary, it has served as a valuable organizing principle for many aspects of scientific knowledge. Scientific research based on an underlying reductionist philosophy has enabled scientists to arrive at syntheses between some areas of knowledge and has been a key engine of scientific progress. For example, the successful unification of the seemingly diverse areas of electricity and magnetism into what we now call electromagnetism would not have been possible unless scientists were driven by the need to try and understand both by unifying them. All that is being stated here is that reductionism cannot serve as a basis for evaluating the relative merits of different branches of knowledge embedded in a hierarchy of truth.

The general reductionist goal of explaining one discipline by using the theories of a discipline that works with a smaller scale has been unsuccessful. While there has been some sharing of concepts and results across the boundaries, the disciplines remain stubbornly distinct and largely independent. This is true even for disciplines that, to the non-scientist, seem extremely closely related, such as nuclear and particle physics.

However, the failure to make significant progress in solving the scientific boundary problems is never perceived as a crisis, or even an anomaly, for reductionism. Instead, this failure to resolve these boundary problems usually is blamed on a lack of ingenuity, on the lack of sufficient personnel to tackle what are admittedly hard problems, and on inadequate technology. It is believed that, given the right resources and sufficient ingenuity, the problems will be solved. This presents yet another source of problems to which scientists can devote their talents, thus continuing the process of normal science.

PART II

CHAPTER SIX

AN ALTERNATIVE MODEL OF SCIENTIFIC PROGRESS

Full many a gem, of purest ray serene,
The dark unfathomed caves of ocean bear;
Full many a flower is born to blush unseen,
And waste its sweetness on the desert air.
— "Elegy Written in a Country Churchyard,"
Thomas Gray

The apparent intractability of the boundary problem between scientific disciplines is not due solely to technical difficulties but may be a consequence of the way science has developed. Indeed, given the nature of scientific knowledge and its evolution, the boundary problem always will be insoluble.

Kuhn (1970) argues that the evolution of scientific theories is analogous to that of the evolution of life. According to Darwin's theory of natural selection, change in organisms occurs through random mutations; and there are potentially an infinite number of mutations that can occur at any time. Not all possible mutations will occur; and of those that do, only those that have some preferential advantage for survival in the environment that exists *at that time* will survive. All the rest will die out.

It is important to remember that evolution is not goal-directed. There is no scientific reason to believe that human beings and all the other living things on our planet right now were the ultimate goal of the evolutionary process that began in the primordial soup. Instead, we are just the accidental by-product of a large number of random mutations. It is quite conceivable that we could have arrived at a different end-point, though we may not be able to envisage it in all its details. The reason that this particular chain occurred out of all the possible ones was due to chance and to the complex interplay between each organism and its environment at any given time. Even making such a distinction between an organism and the environment is an oversimplification. The organism is part of its environment; and when the organism changes, the environment changes, too. Thus the question of which of the many mutations of an organism will survive is not a question that can be answered once for all time. A mutation that has no chance of survival in one era could well be the most favored one if it occurs a million years later.

In much the same way, according to Kuhn, the success of any new scientific theory in gaining acceptance depends on the scientific environment that exists at the time that the theory is created. In turn, the successful theory also determines the future scientific environment. At each branch on its road to progress (where a branch represents a period of crisis), the scientific community determines which of the competing scientific theories best solve the immediate problems confronting it. It then adopts that theory as the best, and all other competitors perish. This also changes the environment of scientific knowledge because it creates a new paradigm centered on the victorious theory and within which all new mutations must occur. The character of the scientific community also changes with the environment, because it is the practitioners of the victorious paradigm who are now in control and thus the arbiters of any new challenge.

If the evolution of scientific knowledge is analogous to that of biological evolution, then the state of scientific knowledge that we now have is also the accidental result of many turns taken by the scientific community in the course of history. Thus the state of knowledge that we now have is not necessarily the inevitable result of scientific progress. We are not moving toward a pre-ordained goal. And if the current state of scientific knowledge is but one of many possible equivalent states, then we cannot argue that it is progressing toward the truth, if that concept refers to something unique.

Scientists would argue that the analogy with biological evolution is not exact. One key difference is that for biological evolution the organism is part of the environment, so that changing the organism also changes the environment. Thus the success of a mutation depends both on its nature and when it occurs. However, the "environment" that determines the success of a scientific theory is what scientists call "nature," a word they use to connote something that is both abstract and objective, consisting of the principles or laws that drive the physical world, as well as its fundamental unchanging constituents. Nature, in this sense, does not change along with changes in our knowledge of it. Thus, in the competition of rival theories for acceptance, the time of occurrence of the competition should be irrelevant. The better theory should ultimately win.

This does not mean that, in the short run, incorrect theories will always lose or that other, subjective factors do not play a role. The social and historical context always plays an important role in the generation of new ideas and their acceptance. If that context is favorable, an idea will flourish and gain adherents. If not, the idea will fade into obscurity or (as in the case with Galileo) be put down with some severity. In the long run, incorrect theories will collapse under the weight of their own contradictions because they will prove themselves to be incompatible with a fixed and unchanging nature. Correct theories will eventually win.

In subsequent chapters I will examine how quantum physics and theories of learning view this same issue of whether nature is an objective entity that is unaffected by our knowledge of it. For the present, I will argue that even conceding that nature is an unchanging entity does not guarantee that scientific knowledge is progressing toward a more accurate representation of the truth. We have seen the problems involved in trying to substantiate the belief that science is approaching the truth. We ultimately are forced into a crude form of scientific confirmationism that says that what we are doing must be correct because it "works."

The key issue that must be faced is trying to explain why science works, while at the same time understanding why scientific knowledge may have very little correspondence with nature or truth. There seem to be just two options. The first is that science works because it is true and that the methodological problems with understanding why it is true must be due to as yet undiscovered inadequacies in the arguments of the philosophers. This is the option that probably is favored by most scientists because it seems plausible. The second option is that the philosophers of science are right that there is no guarantee that science is heading toward truth.

The solution to the problem of why science works so well lies in looking more closely at our models of nature and knowledge. It is possible to construct a model of scientific evolution that explains the fact of scientific success while conceding that it may not be taking us nearer to the truth. It must be emphasized at the outset that such models are not susceptible to proof. They are meant to provide a worldview that is as free from internal contradictions as possible and to provide a plausible explanation of historical development. If this model achieves that limited goal, then the model is useful. Before I introduce such an alternative model for the evolution of scientific knowledge, it is necessary to review how scientific models and theories are created.

At any given time, there exist a set of observations that we call "experimental data." Although experiments are not an impartial and objective surrogate for nature, because of the auxiliary hypotheses involved in their interpretation, the phrase still is a convenient label to describe this combination of sense-data and unproblematic background theoretical knowledge. The best theoretical framework of that particular time, which we have called the paradigm, is required to explain satisfactorily most of the data.

But any given theory has an infinite number of predictions that can, in principle, be made within its domain. Similarly, there are an infinite number of experiments that can be performed. Scientists do not randomly select experiments or theoretical calculations to perform. They are not like children casually picking up stones in the hope that one will turn out to be a gem. Scientists have limited time and resources and need to pick and choose their activities very carefully. They attempt only those experiments and calculations that are technically feasible and promise elucidation of the paradigm. Calculations and experiments typically are not carried out if they require tortuous analyses or the use of auxiliary theories that are themselves in a state of crisis or if they require experiments that no one knows how to set up or that no one has the funds or technology to perform.

Even after allowing for this careful selection of experiment and calculations, no theory ever explains *all* the data that fall within its domain. There always will be predictions of the theory that do not agree with experiment. From this set of unexplained data will eventually come the so-called anomalies that are resistant to solution within the rules of the existing paradigm and that eventually, as argued by Kuhn, lead to the crises that result in the overthrow of the dominant paradigm.

Suppose that an experimental result turns up that does not agree with the predictions of Theory A. This is considered an anomaly. If this experimental result is considered an important consequence of the paradigm and if the existence of the anomaly is confirmed by others, strenuous efforts will be made to extend the theory so that the experimental result comes into agreement with the theory. Now suppose that a new, competing theory, Theory B, explains that anomaly and also explains many, but not all, of the other experimental results explained by Theory A. Indeed, while the calculations for some experimental results are straightforward for Theory A, they are extremely difficult for Theory B and have not been attempted. (Recall that we are usually talking about a large number of possible experimental results and that some selectivity is inevitable.) If the original anomaly turns out to be in persistent contradiction with the predictions of Theory A, and if Theory B can explain it and also can explain other results that also are explained by theory A, then Theory B will emerge as the new paradigm.

In addition, as Lakatos argues, Theory B has an even greater chance of acceptance if it also predicts a spectacular new result. That result may have been an experiment that people working with Theory A would not have even considered doing because it did not meet the criteria for worthiness within Theory A.

Note that it is not obvious that Theory B is "better" than Theory A. Theory B does not explain all the data that Theory A explained. (In fact, when they first are adopted, new theories usually explain fewer experimental results than do the theories they replace, simply because they are newer and relatively few people have worked with them.) Theory B may not even address some of the successful predictions by Theory A. Theory B's one major achievement may be that it is able to explain the one anomaly that Theory A could not explain. So there is no objective reason for preferring Theory B over Theory A.

And what of the experimental results that were successfully predicted by Theory A but which are ignored by Theory B because they do not meet that theory's criteria for worthiness? Such experimental results usually fade into obscurity in the textbooks written after Theory B's ascendancy. Meanwhile, the original anomaly is treated as a falsifying experiment for Theory A and the "spectacular new result" is treated as a spectacular new confirming prediction for Theory B.

There probably are other experimental results that are not explained by either Theory A or Theory B. If those results do not meet either theory's criteria for worthiness, the experiments will not be conducted. Even if a third theory, Theory P, explains these results, it will not be considered because it does not address the anomaly that led to the downfall of Theory A. And once Theory B is accepted as the dominant paradigm, the only problems it addresses are those within its own range of worthiness; and if this range does not overlap those of P, then Theory P will never be considered again, though it might be a very worthy theory.

Eventually Theory B will reach its crisis, to be replaced by Theory C, and D, and so on. But this particular chain of evolution depends on the nature of computational and experimental technology at the time that the crisis for Theory A arose. If these resources had been such that other experimental results, the ones explained by Theory P, had caused the crisis, then the evolutionary branch that scientific knowledge would have followed would have been from A to P and along that branch through Q, R, and so on. This would have been a *completely different chain* and would have led to a different understanding of nature than the one we have now.

It is quite possible that the chain that began with Theory B might eventually, at some later time, overlap with the chain that began with Theory P. This is the kind of thing that happened with the heliocentric theory. It surfaced once in 250 A.D., disappeared, and then reappeared in the 16th century, when it succeeded. But there is no guarantee that this will happen. It is more likely that the branches will never overlap and that even though P and its successors may, at a later time, have been more suitable and fruitful theories than whatever currently is being used, they may never come to light. It is quite possible that there are many excellent theories that have never been born or, having been created, are doomed to obscurity purely for the reason that they could not address the particular questions that were of interest *at the time they originated*. The fact that at any given time we have just a few theories competing for supremacy around a few anomalies may mislead us into thinking that we are nearing the truth, when all it may signify is the poverty of our imagination.

It is now time to introduce an alternative model for the growth and evolution of knowledge and scientific theories. This new model adopts ideas from research done in theories of learning, especially those referred to as constructivist models of knowledge (Bloor 1976). In this approach, knowledge is not something that exists independently and that can be transmitted intact from one person to another. Instead, knowledge is something that is freshly constructed in the mind of each person as a result of trying to reconcile sensory experiences with prior knowledge constructions. The sharing of knowledge occurs when we try to negotiate a shared meaning using our differing individual knowledge constructions.

The alternative model of knowledge being proposed here uses the familiar evolutionary tree metaphor, but with a difference. In this case, the tree represents the *evolution of theories*, and time flows upward from the trunk through the branches. Hence the canopy of the tree represents the state of knowledge in *all* disciplines at the present time, while the trunk represents the early theories. In those early days, these separate disciplines were not far apart so that the "two cultures" discussed by C.P. Snow (1964) had not as yet evolved. Philosophy, science, politics, economics, sociology, all were part of the general education and culture of individuals. The narrowness of the trunk symbolizes the close relationships that existed amongst the various disciplines. Although not everyone may have been familiar with all these areas of knowledge, they were presumed to be knowable by everyone. But as time evolved, each discipline developed its own character, language, style, and literature. The common pool of knowledge started bifurcating, like the main branches in the tree. Each branch went its own way, growing more and more distant from its former neighbors.

Within each major discipline, the splits start occurring, with the sciences branching into the life and physical sciences, the latter then branching into chemistry and physics. Within physics the branching continues, creating new subdisciplines. Finally we reach the canopy, which in this model, represents the *present state of knowledge in all fields*. The canopy represents not only all the various current disciplines (the branches), but also the gaps between disciplines and the gaps in our present knowledge.

As the tree grows, the canopy expands. As the size of each branch in the canopy increases, the gaps between the branches also increase. This means that as time goes by, our knowledge overall and within each discipline will increase, but our ignorance also increases. It is quite possible that even as our knowledge increases rapidly, the amount that we do *not* know also increases rapidly. Furthermore, the distance between the disciplines also will increase. Thus the emergence of the two worlds that C.P. Snow deplored many years ago is not only unlikely to reverse itself, it is very likely to grow, with *many* worlds emerging as more and more disciplines become self-contained and esoteric, making themselves unintelligible to everyone except their own practitioners.

The paradigm crises that Kuhn discussed signify not the struggle of right ideas with wrong, but are branch points in each discipline. After each crisis, the scientific community chooses to go along one particular limb; and the decisions that are made at each branch point result in that discipline ending up in a particular small region of the canopy. If, at some branch point in our past, we had chosen a different theory from the one that was selected, then we would have arrived at a different point on the canopy. We might have arrived at one of the regions that we now consider to be a difficult boundary region or a region of ignorance. Our state of knowledge would be different from what it is now, but it would be as valid. It is just that we now would be interested in different questions.

The sum total of knowledge and ignorance (the total size of the canopy) may be finite at any particular time, but it is *increasing* as time increases. This means that knowledge is not something fixed and external that we can acquire and which results in a decrease in ignorance. Instead, all knowledge, scientific and non-scientific, is something that is constructed by acts of human creativity; and both knowledge and ignorance simultaneously increase with time. Hence what we can know in the future depends on what we know now, because it is what we know now that determines what questions we ask and that guides the search for the answers, which in turn creates new knowledge. There is no end point to the search for knowledge. The potential for new knowledge expands as our knowledge increases. In fact, our ignorance increases along with our knowledge.

It is worthwhile to re-emphasize a key point that follows from this model. If at some crisis point in the past, the scientific community had chosen a different paradigm than the one it historically chose (and thus would, under the conventional view, be perceived as making an "error"), all that would have happened is that we would have followed a different path to the canopy and occupied a different region of space on it. Thus science always will appear to "progress," in that it is always acquiring knowledge that is considered better than that which it replaces; but it is not moving inexorably toward a preordained goal, because there is no preordained goal. Thus we can simultaneously accept science as progressing while denying that it is approaching "the truth," for as long as the latter concept is used to signify a unique state of knowledge to the exclusion of all else, then we cannot prove that we are moving toward it. It is more plausible to believe that our present state of knowledge (whatever it may be) is "truth" in that it represents a particular valid and valuable state of knowledge, but there is no *unique* truth.

This still leaves us the question of how we explain that science has enabled us to make such tremendous advances in technology. This puzzle arises because of our assumption that the ability to control things is identical with the depth of our understanding of whatever is being controlled. In other words, we believe that we are achieving greater technological success over our environment because we are getting closer to the truth about how things are. If we disentangle the concepts of truth and control from one another, then the puzzle goes away. Our tremendous scientific and technological success is simply a measure of how well we can control things, especially inanimate objects. But there is nothing that forces us to believe that control over nature can be achieved in only one way and that increasing control implies increasing truth.

Using the tree metaphor again, control is like the ability to shake the tree. We can shake the tree by grasping any particular point on the canopy. The part of the canopy we currently occupy, our current state of knowledge, is what we can grasp now. But we could have shaken the tree by grasping other points, representing alternative states of knowledge. Grasping different points on the canopy will result in shaking the tree in different ways. Some parts of the canopy may be better than others for this purpose; but because we occupy and are aware of just one region, it is not possible to assert that where we are now is the best of all possibilities. Other places on the canopy, representing other "truths," may be even better for the purposes of control. This does not imply that our predecessors made errors in making the paradigm choices they did. It is simply that the choice was not made on completely objective grounds and hence was not inevitable. A different set of circumstances, a slight change in the temporal spacing of events, and we could have ended up with a very different scientific understanding of how the world works from what we have now.

The relationship between different disciplines on this tree has implications for reductionism. Rather than characterize the disciplines in terms of the different size scales they study, they are just different places on the canopy. They will construct their own new knowledge based on where they are now and the interesting questions that the present state of knowledge in those fields has generated. The boundaries between the disciplines may increase or decrease, but whether this happens has less to do with their size scales than with the nature of the questions that are asked in each discipline and the subsequent questions that the answers generate. If two disciplines evolve so that they have common interests, then they will pose similar questions and invent new concepts that will bring them closer together. But this synthesis will occur because of new conceptual development, rather than by a reductionist approach.

There will never be a "theory of everything," and there is no reason to believe that we are close to the "ultimate truth," let alone that particle physics is the closest to it. It also is unlikely that there is a single set of fundamental particles or a single "God particle," as sought by particle theorists. As long as particle physicists are interested in this type of question, they will proceed to reveal layer after layer of substructure, until at some point interest in this type of question, or research funds, or both, will wane. That point may have been reached already.

In the search for knowledge, we have embarked on a quest for which there is no end. We will continue to gather knowledge indefinitely, some of it beneficial, some not so; but the journey will continue forever. This may dismay some people. We like to have all our actions directed toward a specific goal, whether it be noble or ignoble. But a belief in unlimited knowledge can be enormously exhilarating and liberating.

CHAPTER SEVEN

QUANTUM MECHANICS AND OBJECTIVE REALITY

> I think I can safely say that nobody understands quantum mechanics.
>
> — Richard Feynman

Traditionally, scientific research has been based on the belief that there exists an external reality. We call this an "objective reality" or, more commonly, "nature" or "the world." Science, it is believed, seeks to reveal the nature of this reality by determining the fundamental, unchanging constituents that make up this world as well as the laws that govern its evolution. It does this by making measurements of increasing precision and using the results of these measurements to find patterns and relationships among the various measured quantities. The inductive generalizations based on these patterns are referred to as laws, while the models used to explain these patterns are referred to as theories. Scientists do not make these measurements at random, of course. The choice of which measurements to make out of the infinite number of possibilities is determined by the existing paradigm at any given time.

For example, Newton's theory of gravitation, introduced in the latter part of the 17th century, spawned a renewed interest in detailed observations of the motion of planets. The relative simplicity of the planetary system meant that one could carry out a calculation using Newton's laws and make predictions with some confidence. This provided a means of testing the theory, because there was a fairly firm prediction. The simplicity was important because in the days prior to the advent of computers, one had to choose problems that could be tackled using mathematical techniques that could be carried out by human beings. Our present-day sophisticated computational devices and techniques make simplicity a less compelling requirement, though it still is desirable.

In principle, Newton's theory also is capable of explaining the motion of leaves as they flutter down from a tree. But there has never been much interest in making detailed measurements of leaf motion. The reason is that, in this case, there are so many complicating factors (such as wind currents, leaf shapes, temperature, etc.) that no plausible conclusions can be drawn if an experiment fails to agree with theoretical calculations, because any number of poorly understood factors can be invoked to explain the discrepancy. A discrepancy between theory and experiment would result neither in disproving Newton's theory nor in clarifying it. So of the vast number of possible measurements that fell within the domain of Newtonian mechanics, most (such as leaf motion) were not done. As a result, all those branches of knowledge that could have developed from such measurements remained unexplored.

One consequence of the focus on detailed astronomical calculations and observations was the discovery of the anomalous behavior of Mercury. This recalcitrant planet seemed to be moving in a way that was incompatible with the predictions of Newtonian mechanics. Despite the best efforts of scientists of the time, experiment and theory could not be brought into agreement. This later turned out to be one of the key factors used to argue for a paradigm shift from the Newtonian theory of gravity to Einstein's general theory of relativity. As Newtonian mechanics began to become a degenerating research program, the anomalous behavior of Mercury was elevated to that of a critical, falsifying experiment.

Before the shift to Einstein's theory, another anomaly — the inexplicable behavior of the planet Uranus — was resolved within the framework of Newtonian physics by the postulation and discovery of a new planet, Neptune. This was seen as a resounding triumph for Newton's theory. The point is that the final status of an anomaly is determined after the fact by whether there is a transition to a new paradigm (which makes the anomaly a falsifying fact) or whether the old paradigm remains dominant (which makes the anomaly a confirming fact).

We see that, to some extent, the success of Einstein's theory of gravitation was made possible by the fact that Newton's theory happened to address a topic that also was accessible by Einstein's theory. Both theories were suited for the study of planetary motion, and this made it possible to directly compare them. Mercury's motion was thus an experimental data point of the type described in the previous chapter. In contrast, leaf motion was addressed by neither theory. If there happened to be another exceptionally good theory that addressed leaf motion as one of its strengths, it probably could not have displaced Newton's theory because a direct comparison of the two theories would not have been possible.

Up to now, the words "experiment" and "observation" have been used as a kind of shorthand to describe the complex interplay of sense data and unproblematic background knowledge that characterize the results of an experiment. It was assumed that the role of the observer (the person making the observations) was not really important. For example, it was considered immaterial whether the observer was a human or a machine. All that we needed to know about the observer was how accurate the observer was in making the observations. It was assumed that the observed quantity existed *prior* to the observation and what the observer did was to transform the observed quantity from something that was unknown into something that was known. The details of that transformation were immaterial.

We observed in Chapter 2 that all observations carry some level of uncertainty related to the measuring instruments involved, and that this feature has profound implications for the conclusions we legitimately can draw from those observations. In addition, there is another factor that affects our knowledge of the value of a measured quantity. The very act of making an observation often means that the object being measured is *disturbed* by the observation. For example, to measure the age of a tree, you can take a needle-like cylinder of wood from its trunk in order to count the rings. But the tree after the measurement is not the same as the tree before the measurement because it now has a hole in it.

While this problem has long been realized, it used to be assumed that this was a technical matter that could be overcome using more sophisticated technology so that the disturbance could be minimized or even eliminated. Also, though the tree itself was disturbed by the measurement, the quantity of interest (its present age) was not affected. So there was no fundamental problem with assuming that the role of the observer was a rather passive one. But the advent of quantum mechanics in the early 20th century shattered this concept of a passive observer.

Quantum mechanics is one of the biggest scientific success stories of the 20th century. It created a revolution in scientific thinking that still reverberates today. It forms the basis of our understanding of almost all atomic and subatomic phenomena and has proven to be a remarkably robust and successful theory. It is safe to say that the scientific community would find it unthinkable to conceive of an alternative theory that could match quantum mechanics for accuracy and explanatory power. It is important to realize that its explanatory strength lies primarily in the small size scale of subatomic physics, and it has displaced Newtonian mechanics as the theory used in this domain. But using quantum mechanics to analyze everyday events (such as the motion of a car or a thrown ball) results in staggeringly complicated problems that one has no hope of solving. Newtonian mechanics is still the preferred form of attack for such problems.

In the reductionist epistemology, quantum mechanics is perceived to be a more fundamental (and correct) theory than Newtonian mechanics because quantum mechanics deals with a smaller size scale. The theoretical argument has also been made that Newtonian mechanics is an approximation to quantum mechanics, therefore quantum mechanics can claim credit for all the successes of Newtonian mechanics. This is another theory absorption argument, similar in spirit to the claim that Newtonian mechanics is an approximation to Einstein's relativistic mechanics. Kuhn's exposure of the serious problems that exist with such models of theory absorption was elucidated in Chapter 5.

The advent of quantum mechanics also caused a significant change in our understanding of the role of the observer. This change began with Heisenberg's Uncertainty Principle, which asserts that, for some measured quantities (such as the position of an electron), it is impossible to make a measurement without simultaneously disturbing it. In other words, when you measure an electron's position, the result of your measurement is the position of the electron as a consequence of your disturbance, and not its pre-existing value. Hence there is an uncertainty in the measured value. By itself this was not surprising; we already knew that an act of measurement causes a disturbance in the measured quantity. What was surprising was that the uncertainty principle states that this disturbance is not due to human incompetence or the inaccuracy of the measuring instrument (both of which we might hope to eventually overcome) but instead is an intrinsic property of nature that can never be circumvented, however ingenious we or our measuring devices might become. So an uncertainty in the measured position of the electron is unavoidable and we can never know the exact position it had prior to the measurement.

This immediately raises the interesting question of whether 1) the electron actually has a definite pre-existing position prior to the measurement, though we cannot measure it precisely (which is the commonsense, everyday belief that most people will have), or 2) it never had a precise position to begin with and only gets one as a consequence of the act of measurement. Option 1 is what we have been referring to as believing in an objective reality, that whatever exists exists, whether we observe it or not.

Option 2 is somewhat mind-boggling to those of us accustomed to thinking that everything must be somewhere at all times (even if we don't know where) because it implies that objects need not have a definite location in space at all. It also elevates the hitherto lowly observer into an essential player in the process. Hence Option 2 implies that the electron acquires a definite position only as a result of an act of measurement, which means that the observer of the electron *creates* the electron's position and, consequently, that an objective reality does not exist. Is this what actually happens? The answer to this question has profound philosophical consequences that need to be explored.

In classical (Newtonian) mechanics, objective reality was taken for granted; it was assumed that every particle had a definite position and velocity at any given time. Hence if we knew all the forces acting on a particle and we knew its position and velocity at one time, then we would know precisely where it would be at a slightly later time and how fast it was moving then. If we repeated this for all the particles in the universe, then knowing all their positions and velocities at one time would determine where they all would be at a slightly later time, which in turn would determine where they would be at a yet later time, and so forth. So once the universe was created, it then moved inexorably along a pre-ordained path to a pre-ordained conclusion.

Because all complex objects, such as humans, are considered to be just complicated arrangements of elementary particles, this mechanical universe gave rise to a deterministic philosophy in which there was no room for free will. The present was determined solely by the past, and the future depended only on the present. Free will had to be an illusion because, though an individual's conscious actions were determined by the behavior of his or her brain, this in turn was determined by the motions of the elementary particles that composed the brain and that follow deterministic laws.

Although the Newtonian world was on a completely pre-ordained path, this did not mean we could predict the future with any confidence. In order to do that we would have to know the exact positions and velocities of all the particles that currently exist in the universe, know all the forces between them, and then be able to calculate where they will be in the future. This is an impossible task, except in a few isolated systems of very few particles in controlled laboratory conditions. For anything even slightly more complex (such as weather systems), predictions become increasingly difficult and chaotic, and unpredictable behavior sets in very rapidly. So a deterministic universe does not mean a predictable one. The fact that even remotely accurate predictions cannot be made ensured that cherished notions of free will could survive (albeit somewhat precariously) because its existence could not be experimentally disproved.

The only variation allowed in the deterministic model was that some external entity (God) could arbitrarily intervene in the sequence of events to change the motion of the particles. Believers in a god were left with the uncomfortable task of explaining why such an elaborate deterministic structure should be created by the deity and then circumvented arbitrarily. Science and religion were thus on a collision course.

Quantum mechanics throws a wrench into this model of a deterministic universe. The uncertainty principle asserts that it was impossible to know simultaneously the precise position and momentum (and hence velocity) of an object. This ignorance is not caused by technical difficulties, which we might anticipate overcoming someday, but by a law of nature that cannot be overcome at all unless quantum mechanics itself, one of the foundations of modern science, is overthrown. Thus the prediction of the future becomes not merely immensely difficult, it becomes impossible even in principle. This is not an easy idea to accept. Even the physicist Werner Heisenberg, the enunciator of this famous uncertainty principle that now bears his name, said, "I myself have thought so much about these questions and only came to believe in the uncertainty relations after many pangs of conscience, though now I am entirely convinced" (Bell 1987).

This consequence of the uncertainty principle still involves only the prediction of the future. It is still possible that the universe is deterministic even though it may be impossible, even in principle, to predict how it will evolve. This could happen if every particle does have a definite position and velocity and if the uncertainty principle signifies only a fundamental limitation on our knowledge about them.

So let us repeat the key question: Does a particle have a definite pre-existing position and momentum that we cannot measure precisely, or does it have no precise pre-existing position and momentum at all and gets one only as a consequence of the act of measurement? The answer to this question is of profound philosophical importance because it determines if we are living in a deterministic universe or a non-deterministic one.

There was extensive debate on this question in the early days of quantum mechanics as the theory was being elucidated and scientists struggled to comprehend its implications. The scientific community generally came down, somewhat uneasily, on the side of no position or momentum prior to measurement. It arrived at this position indirectly, more from a philosophy of positivism (or scientific agnosticism) rather than from any direct evidence in support of it. The reasoning goes roughly like this: The only quantities that are of relevance (or interest) to science are those that can be measured. Since the uncertainty principle precludes the measurement of a pre-existing exact position, we have to assume that an exact position does not exist prior to the measurement. To say that something exists and then simultaneously assert that we cannot measure it even in principle would be a logical contradiction, since the only way we prove that something exists is by being able to measure it.

This conclusion is not arrived at without some misgivings, because it seems to fly in the face of our experience. After all, scientists are always talking about the path an object takes in going from one point to another. It could be argued that a path is nothing more than an infinite sequence of closely spaced positions in space that an object occupies as it goes from one location to another. Hence the mere existence of a path seems to imply the existence of an exact position and momentum. But scientists would respond that when they refer to the path of a particle, they simply are employing a heuristic device to aid investigation and provide insight, and the concept of path can be eliminated in more formal mathematical treatments. In fact, scientists have developed methods of analysis that avoid the use of a specific path. These alternative descriptions are more abstract and are couched in the language of probabilities. In order to communicate more easily with one another and the public, scientists invoke classical, intuitive notions of exact positions and moments; but they are not really committed to believing in their existence. Thus the notion of free will can be salvaged because quantum mechanics has undermined strict determinism and reintroduced an element of randomness and unpredictability into the world.

This question of whether the universe is deterministic was of great interest to Einstein. It is fairly well known that Einstein expressed some reservations about quantum mechanics, but it is wrongly asserted that he did so out of a naive and dogmatic insistence that the universe must be deterministic. His frequently quoted statement, "I shall never believe that God plays dice with the world," is often taken to mean that he felt that quantum mechanics was wrong simply because it implied that probabilities were the best one could hope for in answers to questions posed about nature.

While Einstein's early reservations about quantum mechanics may have been due to his beliefs about determinism, his later unease had more subtle causes. He was disturbed because he saw clearly that if quantum mechanics is correct and provides the most complete description possible, then it also denies the existence of an objective reality. After all, if an object does not have a definite position before a measurement, then the properties of particles (such as momentum and position) are created by the act of measurement by an observer. The observer, who hitherto had been just a conduit for receiving information, now becomes an active part of the quantity being measured.

This bothered Einstein immensely, possibly because his own highly successful theory of relativity had built on a long-standing tradition of science in providing a mechanism for an observer-independent description of the world. His unease at this new-found importance of the observer is picturesquely illustrated by a statement he made while walking with a colleague on a clear moonlit night. Einstein suddenly turned toward his companion and asked, "Does the moon exist even when I'm not looking at it?" A negative answer seemed unthinkable to him, so he felt that this particular aspect of quantum mechanics was a weakness that made the theory incomplete. In other words, he felt that there must be some hitherto unknown feature of quantum mechanics that, when uncovered, would resolve this problem of the absence of an objective reality (Bernstein 1991).

This particular issue is interesting because of the surprising way the various protagonists lined up along its dividing line. Einstein has been identified in the public's eye as the man who turned all our conventional notions about the world upside down. As a result of his theories, notions of time and space changed from their familiar, everyday meanings and became fluid concepts that behave in strange ways that are hard to comprehend by lay people. Einstein's name became almost synonymous with esoteric knowledge that is counterintuitive to the person in the street. But on this particular issue, he was squarely on the side of the general public in believing in the existence of an objective reality, that things exist independently of whether anybody observes them.

In this Einstein was opposed by most other eminent physicists of his time, who believed that quantum mechanics is in fact a complete theory and that hence we were forced to accept that there is no objective reality. In other words, there is no hidden feature of quantum mechanics that, if discovered, will restore objective reality, as Einstein clearly hoped. Actually, the situation is a bit more complicated than that. Most physicists today seem to shy away from the disturbing conclusion about the absence of objective reality except when contemplating those very few cases involving experiments whose interpretation directly involves quantum mechanics. But this can be done only for simple microscopic systems. In their everyday lives, or in dealing with the large objects of everyday life, they act as if an objective reality exists. The physicist John Bell observed wittily that you can measure the extent of this internal conflict by the large number of physicists who believe that quantum mechanics is a complete theory but yet purchase life insurance policies (Bell 1987).

Although physicists believe that quantum mechanics represents the best picture we have of the world, the theory can be used to calculate results for only a relatively few laboratory experiments involving very few particles. The vastly greater number of everyday phenomena involve billions of subatomic particles and it is technically impossible to calculate the behavior of such objects using quantum mechanics. Thus we do not have to confront its radical implications about objective reality in our daily lives. For such situations we use classical Newtonian mechanics, which allows for an objective reality. By means of formal and somewhat heuristic arguments, it is claimed that classical mechanics is an approximation of the more correct quantum mechanics and hence all the results of classical mechanics are claimed for quantum mechanics as well. However, because quantum mechanics is believed to be the more correct theory, there can thus be no objective reality *at any level*, though the classical mechanics approximation somehow disguises this fact.

How this process of theory absorption reconciles a theory that denies the existence of an objective reality with one that affirms it is something that is not resolved satisfactorily. It is not even discussed in the formal training of physicists. But the fact that we are forced to use classical mechanics to explain everyday phenomena enables us to avoid confronting the stark issue of how to deal with the seeming objective reality of our everyday lives while still believing that quantum mechanics is a complete theory. The problem is like a dark secret stored away in the closet, taken out only when we actually have to.

Einstein, ever seeking unity and coherence and thus unhappy with this ambiguous state of affairs, tried to pose the conflict in the starkest possible terms in order to force the physics community to come to terms with this problem. In a celebrated paper

written in 1935, Einstein and two co-authors proposed a hypo-
thetical experiment (Einstein, Podolsky, and Rosen 1935). The
EPR paper, as it has come to be known, showed that if such an
experiment were ever done, then the result, whatever it was,
would require that one and only one of the following two
assumptions could be correct: either 1) quantum mechanics is not
a complete theory; or 2) there is no such thing as an objective
reality and some signals can travel faster than the speed of light.
Both options were unpalatable because each violated some cherished belief among physicists. The EPR paper guaranteed that
something precious had to be yielded, a fact that caused some
consternation at that time.

There has never been any doubt that the EPR paper is correct
in its claims. The only dispute is about which of the two options
should be chosen. Einstein lucidly and correctly argued that no
experiment done to date in 1935 excluded either option. So any
choice about which option should be adopted had to be made on
the basis of taste and preference, rather than being strictly determined by experiment. Since the theory of relativity, which he had
been so instrumental in developing (and which was well established by then) argues strongly against anything traveling faster
than the speed of light, he said that the first option was the explanation he preferred. He said that he preferred to believe in an
objective reality and to view quantum mechanics as incomplete.

It is important to note that Einstein did not assert that quantum
mechanics was wrong. He was saying that it was correct only as
far as it went, but it had to be the precursor to a more complete
theory that would not deny the existence of an objective reality or
propose signals traveling faster than the speed of light. That latter option, said Einstein (the master of the sound bite before that
phrase had even been coined), would be tantamount to believing
in a "spooky action-at-a-distance." In Einstein's view, since no
experimental result existed at that time that compelled you to
choose one of the options, the choice had to be made on philosophical grounds. He felt that believing that the theory of quantum mechanics was not complete did less violence to

commonsense ideas of the world than did denying the existence of an objective reality.

Unfortunately, there seemed to be no way at that time, or even in the future, of actually testing whether he was correct in his choice of which option was faulty. It was hard to see how to even set up an experiment along the lines suggested by EPR. All the experimental tests the scientists could think of at that time seemed to predict the same result whichever option one took to be correct. Hence there seemed to be no experimental way of distinguishing between the two options.

It is interesting that, despite the absence of any conclusive experimental evidence either way, the physics community as a whole disagreed with Einstein and believed almost unanimously that quantum mechanics was complete, though it is not clear how many of them were actually aware that they were thus automatically abandoning the notion of objective reality. Their choice was not made on experimental grounds, as required by a strict epistemology of falsification, because no such determining experiments existed at the time. Instead, the choice seems to have been based on the belief that quantum mechanics is such a phenomenally successful theory that it cannot be improved and thus cannot possibly be incomplete (which is a form of confirmatory epistemology). If not for the great prestige of Einstein, it is possible that the viewpoint espoused by him would have disappeared more completely than it did, though it should be again emphasized that there was no experimental evidence whatsoever for rejecting it.

In 1963, John Bell rescued the EPR argument from relative obscurity with an ingenious paper showing that it was possible to design an experiment that could actually put Einstein's view to the test and distinguish between the two possibilities (Bell 1987). Bell's Theorem (or Inequality), as it has come to be known, provoked a flurry of interest in doing experiments to test it; but the technical difficulties were formidable, and it was hard to get unambiguous results. Finally a group in France, led by Alain Aspect, managed to carry out a fairly rigorous experiment. The

result was arrived at in 1982, almost 20 years after Bell's suggestion and nearly 50 years after the EPR paper (Aspect, Dalibard,
and Roger 1982).

The results seem to show that quantum mechanics is complete
and that Einstein was wrong in his choice of which option is correct. The Aspect experiment, while notable and interesting, did
not ruffle any feathers because it did not throw quantum mechanics from the perch it has occupied for the last 70 years as one of
the most successful and dominant paradigms of science. In more
recent years, other researchers have performed even more intricate experiments that seem to support Aspect's findings, thus further cementing the belief that quantum mechanics is complete.

There are two interesting observations that can be made about
the EPR-Bell-Aspect saga. One is that the physics community
firmly believed in the completeness of quantum mechanics for
nearly 50 years even in the absence of any experimental evidence,
thus supporting Kuhn's view that scientists can and do make paradigm choices for subjective reasons.

The other and more crucial point is that the final result that
quantum mechanics is complete means that the existence of an
objective reality is *not* allowed by the best theory we have to date,
namely quantum mechanics. The existence of objective reality
implies a clear distinction between a fundamentally passive
observer and the reality that is being observed. Instead, what is
now asserted is that reality is brought into being by the interac-
tion between the observer and the observed. So we cannot simply
say that more knowledge brings us closer to the truth by giving
us a more complete description of an already existing reality.
Instead, knowledge (which comes in the form of experimental
results, which are themselves theoretical constructs) *creates* the
reality.

Knowledge is synonymous with reality. What exists is what we
know, no more and no less. Increased knowledge does not carry
us toward reality, or truth. As knowledge expands, reality expands
with it. This conclusion is not easy to accept. It is counter to what
we always believed about nature and our role in it. But it seems

to be forced on us by the results of our understanding of what knowledge is and by the dominant paradigm of today, quantum mechanics.

It should be emphasized that probably not many physicists will be aware of all the implications of the Aspect result for the notion of objective reality. When the Aspect results were reported, the reports emphasized that the experiments showed that the conventional beliefs about quantum mechanics were valid and that Einstein's misgivings were unfounded. Both these things are correct, and it is undoubtedly newsworthy when Einstein is found to be wrong. Glossed over was the more dramatic conclusion that an inevitable consequence of this result was its confirmation that we no longer had objective reality.

It is almost as if physicists were ignoring the fact that they made a bargain that they could either accept quantum mechanics as a complete theory or retain a belief in the existence of an objective reality, but not both. Apart from a few physicists who are interested in the philosophical foundations of quantum mechanics, most physicists probably still believe that they can have their cake and eat it too, that quantum mechanics can be thought of as a complete theory and that there still can be an objective reality. Such a desire is understandable. Giving up belief in an objective reality, so long a solid foundation of our belief structure, is profoundly disturbing. If that goes, what belief is safe?

An early anonymous reviewer of this manuscript responded to this point about quantum mechanics and objective reality in a way that is fairly typical of the uneasy and ambivalent attitude most scientists have on this topic. The reviewer said, "The fact is that most of the scientific community, *despite the implications of quantum mechanics,* believes in an objective reality, and the full answer to this apparent conflict is not yet available" (emphasis added). However, as Einstein showed in 1935, you cannot have it both ways. The only way you can recover objective reality is by rejecting quantum mechanics.

The non-scientist may wonder why physicists cling so strenuously to the troublesome notion that quantum mechanics is a complete theory. After all, it is *only* a theory. What would be the harm in assuming that there is a better theory lurking somewhere, to be discovered in the future, one that allows for the existence of an objective reality? The fact that the scientific community does not do this supports Kuhn's contention that the scientific community always assumes that its current paradigms are the best and refuses to concede the existence of a better one until the old one enters a period of crisis. And as long as this issue is not perceived as a crisis for quantum mechanics and it continues as a progressive research program, it will remain the dominant paradigm.

It is not that scientists are complacent about this lack of objective reality. It is just that this idea is hard to accept. Richard Feynman, one of the most innovative and imaginative physicists of the 20th century whose own research produced spectacular successes for quantum mechanics, summed up the feelings of many scientists on the issues raised by John Bell and EPR when he said, "I cannot define the real problem, therefore I suspect that there's no real problem, but I'm not sure there's no real problem" (Feynman 1982).

But there is a real problem here, and it will not go away. Cornell physicist David Mermin has written extensively on the EPR paradox and has, along with John Bell, been partly successful in keeping the issue alive. He quotes a colleague as saying, "Anyone who is not bothered by Bell's Theorem must have rocks in his head" (Mermin 1985).

PART III

CHAPTER EIGHT

SCIENCE AND SCIENCE EDUCATION

Four legs good, two legs bad.
— *Animal Farm*, George Orwell

Policy makers insist on the need for a population that is scientifically literate (and numerate) as an essential ingredient for the well-being of a nation. They argue that in a world that is becoming increasingly technical and complex, the future workforce will need a level of scientific, mathematical, and computational sophistication that is far in excess of what their parents needed. The days are gone when a student could drop out of school, obtain a job in the local factory without any further training, and still realize a middle-class lifestyle. Now even a high school diploma is not enough. A student should have a college degree (or at least a few years of college-level education) and specialized training in some area if he or she is to get a job that pays anything close to what his grandparents could earn with their more rudimentary education. Thus there are repeated calls from all sides for programs that emphasize and increase science and mathematics education at all levels from kindergarten through college. The general public is constantly exhorted to pay more attention to science and the scientific education of their children. The generally low level of scientific literacy among the public is periodically deplored.

Paradoxically, despite all these exhortations about the importance of science, one of the main complaints of science teachers is that it is exceedingly hard to motivate students to learn science because students do not see it as relevant to their futures. Why is it that so many students do not seem to understand what everyone says: that knowing science is important? Are they so obtuse that they are willing to indulge in self-destructive behavior by ignoring the very subjects that could lead them to highly rewarding careers, despite the pleas of parents, teachers, and national leaders?

The causes of this seemingly anomalous behavior have been extensively researched, and many plausible reasons have been put forward to explain this apathy. I will not review that literature but instead point out one possibility, which is that the case for the importance of a knowledge of science for personal economic well-being is not quite as compelling as it seems on the surface. While it is true that modern technology requires a high level of knowledge of science and that careers that use these high-level skills are increasing very rapidly and are some of the most financially rewarding, it also is true that the actual number of such jobs in absolute terms is very small and is likely to remain so for the foreseeable future. The largest employers will continue to be those in the service sector, all providing jobs (such as shop-assistants, waiters, and secretarial services) that require relatively low levels of scientific expertise to carry out (Bracey 1992).

Most students are quite good at weighing their career odds and spending their time accordingly. Those who come from environments that bring them repeatedly into contact with people who have relatively lucrative and prestigious careers, such as doctors, lawyers, engineers, and scientists, are likely to believe that they, too, have a good chance of getting into this narrow range of well-paid professions; hence they are more likely to invest time and effort on learning science, however poorly it is taught. They may not enjoy the experience or appreciate the relevance of the science they are learning in school, but they are willing to suspend judgment and make the effort out of the belief that there will be a payoff sometime in the future.

But students who come from environments where almost everyone is involved in low-skill occupations that seem to require no scientific knowledge might see things quite differently. They might well feel that their chances are small of ever overcoming the educational, financial, and social barriers that face them on their path to a financially rewarding career. In that context, the seeming irrelevance of much of school education (particularly science education) to their daily lives is sufficient reason to not devote much effort to it.

In one of my many visits to observe the science teachers I work with, I visited an eighth-grade science classroom in a Cleveland middle school in which the population was primarily from low-income households. The science teacher pointed out two boys who were sitting together. She said that both students seemed bright but neither one was motivated to study science. I joined both of them at their table while they went through the motions of doing the science exercise assigned to them. It was clear that they received no joy from what they were doing. I was interested in their attitudes to science and asked them about their career plans. One student said that he was already a fairly good auto mechanic and cook; he had relatives who worked in those occupations, and was learning these two crafts from them. He usually spent his summers and spare time working at these two jobs in order to improve his skills. He felt he could make a fairly good living in either occupation, and he simply did not see where science played any role in either choice. He felt he could do just as well with the knowledge he gained outside the classroom. The other student wanted to be a pediatrician and, though he knew that science would be useful somehow, he could not say why. For him, going to science classes at school was simply a hoop that he had to jump through in order to get into a high-income career. But he said that his chances of being able to afford college were zero and that his only hope of getting a college education was to get a basketball scholarship. To that end, he was devoting most of his time to getting better at basketball, even if his schoolwork suffered.

Both students were making rational choices based on what they perceived as realistic assessments of their own futures. They were neither stupid nor indulging in self-destructive behavior. What was interesting was their view of science. Both students clearly viewed science as a specific body of knowledge that served a specific purpose. If their own perceived futures did not include those purposes, they did not see why they should spend time studying it. The hope that their futures would require such knowledge would, in their view, be as likely as winning the lottery. Only an exceptionally far-sighted, ambitious, and trusting child, supported by similar family members, would make such an investment. Hence it should not be surprising that few Horatio Alger-type stories emerge from such bleak surroundings. The majority of students reject science as a viable choice and opt instead to spend their energies on those pursuits that realistically promise a brighter financial future.

One might expect that children would want to study science for its own sake, because of the satisfaction they would derive from having their curiosity satisfied. After all, little children are immensely curious. They do not need much prodding to ask questions about the world around them. As many exasperated parents can testify, children can be insatiable in their quest for knowledge, following one question with another with no seeming end to their curiosity. But this wonderfully inquisitive nature of children seems to disappear after a few years of schooling, rarely to return. Their perception of science becomes that it is dull, formulaic, esoteric, and purely classroom-centered, unrelated to anything that is going on in the real world they experience every day.

The reason that science is seen as so irrelevant by most students is that it is taught, and hence perceived, as a specific body of information that has been distilled and tested down through the ages and found to be true. The goal of science education seems to be to transmit as much of this information as possible into the mind of the student in as intact a form as possible. Such an approach emphasizes "facts" (measured quantities) and "theories and laws" (inferences drawn from these measured quantities). Unfortunately, science is not taught in a way that incorporates the scientific method as a continuous and intrinsic part of the teaching and learning process. We seem to have ignored Alfred North Whitehead's warning: "In training a child to activity of thought, above all things we must beware of what I call 'inert ideas' — that is to say, ideas that are merely received into the mind without being utilized, or tested, or thrown into fresh combinations" (1929, p. 1)

A deep understanding of facts and theories may not be required in the everyday lives of most people, and hence science may be irrelevant in some sense. But the scientific method is an extremely useful and transferable skill that should be valuable in all of life's activities.

But how best to integrate scientific content and method is not easy to determine. Part of the problem lies with science textbooks, which tend to determine much of science teaching practices. Most of them begin with an introductory chapter "explaining" the elements of the scientific method by describing the making and testing of hypotheses, the importance of measurements, and the rules by which inferences can be made. But once these seeming formalities are out of the way, the textbooks proceed to lay out the facts, laws, and theories in such a way as to make them almost indistinguishable from one another. All of them are presented as received wisdom handed down through the ages, as if all the interesting scientific discoveries were made by clever people who lived long before us. The teaching method promoted by these textbooks seems to be based on the belief that telling students how *other* people successfully practiced the scientific method and having students retrace those paths will give the students themselves an understanding of the scientific method and the ability to apply it in other situations.

This teaching strategy does not work. Most students do not see the point of learning the lists of facts and refrain from doing so. Those who do make the effort still develop poor scientific skills. They do not really understand the scientific method and cannot apply it in other situations. Students find it hard to distinguish between observation and inference, correlation and causation, induction and deduction, and such other basic features as paradigm creation and refinement, all of which characterize the scientific approach to solving problems. One has only to look closely at the quality of private and public discourse in our lives to observe the absence of these skills. The only people who seem to acquire these skills are the very few whose paths in life happen to take them into activities, such as research of any kind, that require learning and using these abilities.

The scientific method cannot be learned content-free. It cannot be taught simply as a method apart from the disciplines that gave rise to it. So scientific facts and theories must be taught, but only in such a way that students also experience the scientific method firsthand.

Much research has gone into understanding the reasons for this failure in education. It is beyond the scope of this essay to review the immense body of literature around the subject of why Johnny and Jane allegedly cannot read, write, or count. Poor textbooks, poor curricula, and inadequately trained teachers are some of the reasons that usually are given. Other people blame a seemingly increasing anti-science mood among the general public as the main cause, and this view is examined further in the next chapter. Yet others, with a somewhat more apocalyptic vision, lay the blame on what they perceive as a general disintegration of society. All these criticisms have different degrees of validity, and efforts have been made to improve the situation in some areas. However, we should be wary of jumping to the popular and easy conclusion that this is a recent phenomenon and that the situation was better in some previous "golden age." There is considerable evidence not only that is this not true, but that a plausible argument can be made that educational levels, in a general sense, have improved over time, so that the problems of science education outlined above have a very long history (Berliner and Biddle 1995).

The problems with science education have existed for a long time, but their adverse consequences are being highlighted only now. An important component of the problem may lie in the popular worldview of scientific knowledge. If we believe, as so many do, that the scientific path that we have followed so far is directed toward the truth in some absolute sense, then it is perfectly appropriate to teach science in the way it usually is taught, as the handing down of received wisdom. It also becomes a reasonable strategy to have students trace the path that the scientific community has followed in the development of the theories that we now believe to be true. Any deviations from this straight and narrowing path are used only to illustrate the correctness of what we know now. So Aristotelian mechanics is taught just sufficiently to show its inadequacy when compared with Newtonian mechanics. Newtonian mechanics is valued for its practical utility but also is asserted to be incorrect when compared with the correct theories of relativity and quantum mechanics. The process continues within these subdisciplines, the path becoming narrower and narrower as we progress; and the student is guided carefully along the path to truth that has been traversed by many before him.

From the point of view of the beginning science student, however, what lies ahead of him or her is a long and tedious process of learning established and well-known material. When a student is given a science problem to work on, the student knows that many thousands, if not millions, of students before him have worked the identical problem. It is just his turn. The only challenge for the student lies in showing the teacher that he, too, has learned what is already well known. Any exploratory wandering off the standard path is discouraged by the teacher as a waste of time because it is bound to lead to error. After all, we know what is correct. What is the point in letting students reinvent the wheel? The only permitted wanderings are to view briefly those false trails that already have been selected as paradigm-shifting events and whose sole purpose is to show us why we should stick to the current main path.

Teachers shepherd students of science carefully along the same well-worn and predictable path. The students are guided by different teachers at different stages, but the road they must take is well-defined. While this pilgrimage toward the shrine of current knowledge is progressing, students fall by the wayside at different stages along the path. The few who persevere to the very end are rewarded with a Ph.D. and (finally!) have the opportunity to contribute to the creation of new knowledge. However, they still are not totally free. At this stage, too, the range of activities is severely curtailed by the limits of the current dominant paradigm and its rules of operation. As Kuhn points out, anyone who wanders outside the perimeters of the current paradigm and does not accept its premises has effectively, in the view of the scientific community, ceased to practice science. This can be quite a deterrent to really novel ideas.

Should we be surprised that most students find this a somewhat bleak prospect and are not enthusiastic about it? Compare this with other activities in which children indulge, such as writing an article or story, composing a poem or song, or creating a drawing or painting. These acts are done spontaneously by children, and they have an immense pride in their accomplishments. They rightly feel that they have created something that no one has created before and that it has originality and value, at least in their own eyes. They can experience the excitement of using their imaginations, and this is evidenced by the fact that children love to display their artwork for all to see.

On the other hand, science, as usually experienced by students, can offer none of this exhilaration of creativity. How often do we see children bursting with pride at being able to solve a science homework problem and showing it off to their family and friends or sticking it on the refrigerator? The best we seem to be able to do is to disguise the intrinsic lack of creativity involved in learning science by employing technology to distract the students. We now have glossy textbooks with wonderful graphic illustrations, spectacular demonstrations, high-technology laboratories, and computers. All these innovations undoubtedly eliminate some of the tedium of learning, as well as offer students the impression that they are at the cutting edge of learning. But it is an illusion. The students are merely watching sideshows along the beaten path of science. Although these sideshows use knowledge garnered at the frontiers, the students themselves are not being creative. To avoid any misunderstanding, I emphasize that I am not trying to imply that we should have dull textbooks and eliminate modern technological aids. All I am saying is that they can never be a substitute for the emotional and intellectual stimulation that comes with real creativity. And students know this.

The prevailing model of education seems to be based on the belief that all students start with many erroneous beliefs about how the world works and have just a vague glimpse of the truth. As they progress along the path, they approach the truth by seeing how scientists got rid of errors. Along the way, students begin to drop off the trail as they pursue other activities. This usually happens when students either will not or cannot stay on the trail and keep wandering off the path despite the best efforts of their teachers to keep them in the fold. Most of the dropouts from science occur early. Many students may formally continue to enroll in science classes, but they have mentally rejected science as an interesting activity. Only the ones who stay to almost the very end (at least through graduate school) are considered by science practitioners to be truly knowledgeable about their chosen field.

It is disturbing that some teachers see this progressive attrition in the number of students who pursue science at higher levels as a natural, and even desirable, phenomenon. Such people tend to believe that there is something intrinsic to science that makes its knowledge accessible to only a select few. They believe that one of the goals of education is to sort out students into those who can do science and those who cannot, even though they cannot convincingly articulate any special quality in people (or in science, for that matter) that makes this difference. I have seen no convincing evidence to support this attitude and view the steady elimination of students as a tragedy for science. We may be weeding out some of the most creative and imaginative minds.

Physicist H.R. Crane derided the traditional approach to teaching science by describing what a murder mystery novel would be like if it took the same attitude as physics textbooks take. The first chapter would start with an explanation of the legal system, the second would deal with forensic science, the third would describe how police investigative agencies work, and so on, until finally, in the very last chapter, the dead body would be discovered. The solution of the mystery would then be left to the reader as a home-work exercise in the belief that the reader by now should have all the information and skills to solve it. But how many readers would be willing to wade through all the tedious preliminaries on the basis of a promise of a challenge at the very end? Not many. And only a small percentage of the few who actually make it to the end would have acquired the necessary skills to solve the mystery.

One of the frequent complaints I have heard about college and high school students is that, by and large, they are not risk-takers, that they are interested only in the answer and do not want to think for themselves. The claim is made that students want to be told exactly what they need to do and learn and then to be tested by being asked to do the very same thing. Any teacher who vio-lates this unwritten rule is perceived as being unfair. It has been suggested that there is an unwritten and unspoken contract that exists between students and teachers — students will accept bad teaching in which they learn little in exchange for bad examina-tions that require little real learning.

What should be surprising is not that older students have this negative attitude to science, but that it is not much worse. After all, year after year, children are given the impression that what science they already thought they knew is either of no value or is wrong, and all their exploratory speculations are discouraged unless they happen to fall within the currently accepted para-digm. It is inevitable that students will end up thinking that there is no use in expending any creative energy, because almost every-thing of any value is already known by their teacher or someone else. If you do make the effort and are certified to be correct, you still have not done anything new, whereas if you are wrong, you have failed. So why not wait until some authority tells you what is going on and what you should do? It is a far more efficient way of spending one's time than thrashing around in useless activities that are likely to lead nowhere. This is a rational response by stu-dents to this model of knowledge.

One promising development is the current research on how students learn. Students are not ignorant, empty vessels into which knowledge can be poured intact. The vessels are full, in fact, of quite complex belief structures that students have about the world around them. These belief structures are created in students' minds even in the absence of any formal teaching because human beings need to have theories of how the world works. Hence all of us, often without consciously realizing it, construct theories that explain to our own satisfaction why and how things work the way they do. These beliefs are quite robust (since they have been built from our own experiences and are our own creation) and we are not going to discard them easily. Simply telling students what the correct theories are has little impact on them because their own theories have been quite functional; and the students have been given no reason, other than the word of an authority figure, to reject their theories. For a few students, the authority figure's assurance is sufficient persuasion. Such students tend to be the ones who succeed in the traditional science education. But for many, the teacher's explanations of why things behave the way they do has no personal relevance. Students may acquiesce in order to avoid trouble, but they revert to their own beliefs as soon as the teacher's influence is removed.

Modern teaching methods, based on an alternative, constructivist model of learning, emphasize that one has to start from where the students are and get them to explore the consequences of their existing beliefs as a precursor to learning the theories you want them to learn. It is held that students must experience for themselves why their own theories are inadequate before they become willing to accept new theories. They must learn how to make judgments between two competing theories, with all the logical problems that this entails. The transformation that must take place in the mind of an individual student in order for real learning to occur is similar to the revolution that causes the scientific community to shift its allegiance from an old paradigm to a new one. The paradigm shift does not occur simply because of the appearance of a good new idea or the assurances of an authority figure. There has to be a crisis in the old paradigm, and good teaching requires the creation of such crises in the mind of the student.

Constructivist pedagogy (Brooks and Brooks 1993) asserts that knowledge is not something that is stored in textbooks, other literature, and the minds of experts and can be transmitted intact into the mind of the learner. Instead, all knowledge is something that is constructed in the mind of the learner in response to outside stimuli. In this model, the learner always has a set of prior beliefs that have worked well. The only reason that this knowledge will undergo any change is if the learner experiences something that cannot be explained by his or her own existing belief structure. This causes a mental disequilibrium that goes away only when the learner constructs a new theory that can absorb the new information. In other words, each person has to "reinvent the wheel" in order to achieve a deep understanding. Rather than being considered a waste of time, reinventing the wheel is an important part of the learning process.

Needless to say, a process of completely free inquiry can be an extraordinarily time-consuming learning method because there are many paths that a person can explore. In order to save time, a process of guided inquiry will carefully create experiences that will lead students to conclusions that are in conflict with their prior beliefs and thus toward beliefs that are in agreement with accepted scientific paradigms. Supporters of guided inquiry argue that, though this process still takes longer than simply asserting through lectures, it is more effective because students obtain a much deeper understanding of what they learn.

However, constructivists still believe in right and wrong theories. Although constructivists realize the importance of dealing with existing student beliefs, they still do not value these beliefs as valid forms of knowledge. Some advocates of constructivism even label these prior student beliefs as "misconceptions," and their method of teaching is designed to show students the error of their misconceptions so that they can be led, by successive refinements of their beliefs, to the truth.

Instead of labeling pre-existing student beliefs as "misconceptions," with all the negative connotations that this word evokes, I would prefer to coin a new word, *theoroid*, which better illustrates that the student belief is a real theoretical construct. Just as the term *factoid* is used to denote an item of fact that is disconnected from any meaningful context, a theoroid represents a theory that is perfectly valid in that it explains the phenomena it was designed to serve but is not part of any broader theoretical construct. Theoroids should not be treated as false but as constructs that are valid expressions of knowledge within the domain for which they were designed and as part of the paradigm-developing process. Students should be encouraged to explore their existing beliefs and to view them, not as incorrect or as misconceptions, but as valid paradigms that should be used as springboards for further exploration.

There are many who will be aghast at this suggestion. They will worry that this method of teaching science will result in thousands of students wallowing in what the scientific community considers to be error. They might warn of a catastrophe as we let loose into the world an educational and scientific anarchy that would cause the end of civilization.

Actually, it would be difficult to notice any change at all. What I have described is the *current* situation, and we seem to be coping with it just fine. At present, most students, despite the earnest efforts of their teachers, leave school with beliefs about science that seasoned science practitioners find to be appalling. We have learned to deal with this situation, even if we are not happy about it. What we will gain is giving students the sense that they are a part of the creative process, that the theories they develop and the experiments they do in exploring their paradigms are creating new knowledge, just as any story they write or music they play is creating something new. I believe this new attitude will lead to a rebirth of interest in science because people will revel in the freedom of scientific exploration and paradigm development. This search for new discoveries and the exhilaration in making one is what lies at the heart of the scientific enterprise.

This does not mean that there will be no standard body of scientific knowledge. As I have stated repeatedly, science works because it has provided us with unprecedented control over our environment. There always will be those who want to achieve such control in the quickest possible way. Such people will need to learn the standard paradigms in that area of knowledge. So we will continue to produce physicists, chemists, biologists, doctors, etc. But everyone else could also share in that sense of adventure and creation so lacking in most science education. And their theoroids may take them into new areas of knowledge that may turn out to be useful, or they may not. But the new knowledge that is created will be theirs, with all the pride of ownership and creativity that comes along with it.

It is illustrative to compare the situation in science to that in music or art or language or history or any other organized body of knowledge. While there are clearly identifiable authorities and an accepted canon of work that is respected in these other fields, lay people also can do original work that contributes to these fields. More important, even novices in these fields can feel a sense of creation and success, which is the ultimate stimulus to further effort. In music, for example, this freedom to create has been the very source of its vigor. People continually experiment with new musical instruments and styles, enriching our culture.

I can distinctly remember, when teaching myself to play the guitar, the first time I could switch between three different chords without an interminable pause for finger placement between each change. I experienced such a rush of success and creativity that I immediately started playing songs. These songs would have been considered terrible by serious musicians, but no one could deny that it was music in some loose sense of the word. And it was my music. If I had wanted to be a professional musician, I would have studied it more formally; but as my interests were elsewhere, my skills stayed at a very low level. I still feel that I am playing music, even though people scatter when I reach for my guitar.

The main thing is that in the process of playing at even a rudimentary level, I have developed an appreciation for music and feel confident that I can evaluate and criticize it, while yet appreciating the knowledge and expertise that seasoned professionals bring to it. Thus one finds in music a complete spectrum of enthusiasts, from the complete novice to the professional, and at each level people are playing and listening to music together and deriving great pleasure from a very creative experience.

The examples can be multiplied. In sports, between the complete beginner and the professional athlete, one finds a whole spectrum of players and observers who play for fun. Such people feel comfortable enough with their knowledge of the game to criticize the professionals. Even though they cannot play at the professional level, they feel entitled to demand explanations from coaches and players for their actions. Similarly, when it comes to language, people spontaneously create new words and even dialects; and these can gain popularity and acceptance even against the opposition from the linguistic establishment. The point is that everyone feels they can develop at least an appreciation for all these activities, and occasionally these non-experts create whole new areas of activity in these fields.

But in science there is a vast wasteland between the professional scientist and the general public. It is as if there was nothing in music between the members of the Cleveland Symphony Orchestra and the middle-school band. There are no spontaneous formations of small groups of people to do science in the way a few people with a little musical expertise get together to jam or others form a softball team or a book club. The general public feels they have nothing to contribute to science, they have no creative input, their opinions are of no value. They feel that new scientific knowledge can be created only by experts, and that all they can do is observe and marvel.

We see the consequences of this belief all around us. People who would feel embarrassed to confess to a total ignorance of language or music state their ignorance of science quite proudly, confident that they are in the overwhelming majority. There is no stigma attached to being scientifically illiterate. Instead of lecturing people and trying to make them feel guilty about their ignorance, we should try to understand why people are so detached from science and feel no desire to be active participants in the endeavor.

The situation is even worse than a general disinterest. Teachers in our elementary and middle schools typically are terrified at the prospect of teaching science. These teachers usually are competent professionals who could, at short notice, be asked to teach history, geography, social studies, and language and would face these subjects with equanimity. But ask them to teach science, and they recoil at the idea. They fear science because they feel they do not know anything about the subject. What they once learned has long since been forgotten. They, too, usually left the path of scientific knowledge at a very early stage. They think that in order to teach science they have to know all the scientific facts and theories and be able to state everything correctly and with authority. They are terribly worried that they will inadvertently teach the wrong thing. They do not value their own scientific knowledge. The result is that we end up with the worst of all worlds. Teachers who are coerced into teaching science quickly gather what scientific facts they can and present them to students with an air of finality as eternal truths. They teach science as inert ideas, as concepts developed by experts that cannot be questioned or challenged. But since the more sophisticated scientific theories require mathematical skills beyond those usually available to students, the theories that they are taught are of a fairly rudimentary nature. When these students come to college, they are confronted by instructors who are specialists in their fields and who effectively tell them to forget what they have learned. Is it any wonder that students feel that science has very little to do with the real world?

This is not to say that there is no public interest in science. The very idea that scientific knowledge is accessible to and can be created by only a few experts at the pinnacle of the discipline has given it a mystique. Thus we have the proliferation of popular books that try to enlighten the public about the more spectacular theories and discoveries that come from the scientific community. We have regular science columns that appear in newspapers and magazines. We have television specials. All this effort is in the service of increased scientific literacy.

While there is agreement that it is desirable to raise the level of scientific literacy among the general public, there usually is very little detailed examination about what we mean by the phrase *scientific literacy*. Most efforts attempt to make people more knowledgeable about advances in science, medicine, and technology, as if scientific literacy parallels what is popularly termed "cultural literacy." Hence literacy is believed to be obtained when people have a broad, though superficial, understanding of the key elements of a subject. Most books and newspaper columns seem to be written with these goals in mind, and a lot of the formal science education in schools is also based on this view. The belief seems to be that if people become familiar with the words and concepts that form the basis of recent scientific developments, they will understand what the scientific enterprise is all about.

While many of these books, articles, and programs are well conceived, their goal seems to be to explain in lay terms the latest version of the truth as perceived by the scientific community. I suspect that while the general public is appreciative of these efforts to explain the latest knowledge at the frontiers of science, these efforts also increase the sense that scientific knowledge is attainable by only a few. Thus, paradoxically, this kind of effort to increase scientific literacy can create a sense of alienation from science. People begin to feel that scientists are a modern-day priesthood who hold the key to the ultimate understanding about the world, and many people resent that. This resentment can give rise to an anti-science sentiment, especially when the views of the scientific establishment come into conflict with those of other collective interests. The long-running battle between naturalists and creationists is a well-known case in point.

The emphasis of science education should not be on a superficial familiarity with the words and concepts of current scientific theories. Instead, it should focus on providing people with a personal experience of creating and modifying paradigms. In other words, the emphasis should shift from what facts people know or should know to helping them to examine more closely why they believe what they believe (Arons 1990). This would create connoisseurs of knowledge, people who have the ability to discriminate between different kinds of knowledge and to judge for themselves which is most useful in any context.

People need to be able to identify what the issues are, to expose fallacious logic, to distinguish between observation and inference, and to decide between competing explanations. They need to know what information is needed to make a judgment and how to set about acquiring that information. Such skills are extremely useful for people going about their daily lives and participating as active citizens in public life. These skills are far more important than acquiring huge amounts of factual information about science. People can acquire facts when they need them.

CHAPTER NINE

SCIENCE AND RELIGION: A POSSIBLE SOLUTION

The Lord God is subtle, but malicious he is not.
— Albert Einstein

Many years ago, while I was an undergraduate student in Sri Lanka, I attended a conference sponsored by an ecumenical organization. The topic was that old staple, "Science and Religion." The purpose of the meeting was to see how to reconcile the seemingly conflicting scientific and religious worldviews. Representatives of the various religions in Sri Lanka (Buddhism, Hinduism, Islam, and Christianity) spoke at the meeting, as did scientists. I cannot recall any of the talks (I suspect that they covered the usual ground that I had heard in many similar conferences) but I distinctly recall overhearing a casual conversation between delegates while in the lobby during a break. A Hindu participant told a Buddhist delegate, "You know, it is the Christians who are always worried about this topic. They are the ones who are worried that science is turning their young people away from religion, and they keep dragging us into these discussions even though it is not a problem for us."

I was struck by this remark because my own experience seemed to confirm its validity. My non-Christian friends were as interested in science as I was, and many of them practiced their religions; but it was only my Christian friends who really agonized over how to bring both aspects of their lives into some convergence. Non-Christians, by contrast, would practice their scientific profession by day and their religion by night (so to speak) and seemingly saw no contradictions. They did not have the same degree of soul-searching as to whether their religious beliefs were compatible with their scientific ones. So the Hindu delegate's observation that this was an issue that mainly concerned Christians was accurate and cried out for an explanation.

The prime problem that confronts Christians who also have an affinity for science is the well-known one that we discussed in the beginning of this book: how to reconcile a belief in the existence of a God who can work miracles (by definition a violation of natural laws) while pursuing science, which seems to require an assumption that nature proceeds according to laws that do not allow for arbitrary violations. According to the orthodox scientific worldview, any seeming violations that do occur are presumed to be due to yet unknown and deeper laws, and thus the target of further research. Christians who are also scientists are always debating the relationship between science and religion, trying to find ways to be faithful to both traditions without being accused of being inconsistent.

The conventional explanation for the Christian's dilemma is to blame it on the religious belief structure. Christianity, it is alleged, created this problem for itself by making sweeping claims about the role of the deity in the working of nature. Historically, Christianity has presumed to know the answers to those questions that science could not explain at any given time, ranging from everyday items (such as how the human body works) to cosmic questions (such as the origins of the universe). This created what some theologians dubbed a "God of the Gaps," whose existence was revealed by the very presence of things that science could say little about. Many features of nature (such as the human eye) are extremely complex and seem to require such delicate fine tuning in order to work as well as they do that it seemed natural to think that their presence could not be explained as the consequence of random chance or natural law. Thus these features were presumed to have been created by a supernatural power, and the function of God seemed to be to explain the scientifically inexplicable. This immediately set Christianity open to conflict with science as the latter's ability and scope for producing plausible explanations kept expanding. The celebrated cases of Galileo and the Scopes trial are examples of how Christians had difficulties incorporating their religious beliefs into areas that were coming under the increasing scrutiny of science. As science advances, creating more and more knowledge and thus decreasing our need for religious explanations, Christianity has been put into a state of constant retreat. The "gaps" of ignorance are narrowing, threatening to squeeze Christianity out completely.

But this cannot be the sole explanation for why Christianity seems to be in greater conflict with science than are other religions. Other religions also make sweeping miraculous claims. The supernatural aspects of Hinduism, Judaism, and Islam, for example, can be quite spectacular, though they differ in detail from those of Christianity. Hinduism, Judaism, and Islam, like Christianity, are theistic religions with an activist God, a position that immediately creates potential for conflicts with science. While Buddhism does not formally require the existence of God, it does postulate a set of laws governing reincarnation that have the potential for conflict with science. So it can be argued that the supernatural (or miraculous) claims of Christianity that form the basis of the long-running conflict with science differ only in degree from those of other religions and cannot be the sole basis of the intense conflict with science in which Christianity constantly seems to find itself embroiled.

In my opinion, the root of the conflict lies neither with scientific knowledge itself nor with the Christian religious belief structure, but with the view of the nature of knowledge that has arisen in Western culture and which forms the common framework for understanding both science and Christianity. In Western popular culture, knowledge is perceived as finite (though large) so that an increase in knowledge is automatically accompanied by a decrease in ignorance. In such a model, it is implied, even necessary, that eventually we will "know everything," and that hence there will be no room for an activist deity. Furthermore, the tremendous growth in knowledge that we have witnessed just in the 20th century has created a sense among some scientists that we already know almost everything important about nature, and that the things that remain to be discovered are relatively few in number and of lesser importance. Some have even proclaimed that we have reached the "end of science" (Horgan 1996). This does not leave much maneuvering room for religion, and many religious believers have long sensed this danger and have vigorously battled scientific progress. Since Christianity is the dominant religion in Western cultures, it is this particular religion that is at the forefront of the science-religion conflict, though the same issues confront other religions.

This sense of already having almost total knowledge about nature is not shared by those who live outside (at least partly) the pervasive influence of Western culture. In Eastern cultures, the more common feeling is that what we know is infinitesimally small compared to the knowledge that exists, and that we are far away from approaching the limits of knowledge. It is believed that we are swimming in a vast ocean of ignorance that gives plenty of room for advances in both scientific and religious knowledge without them coming into conflict with each other. Hence it is felt to be pointless to worry too much about conflicts with science and religion because it is quite conceivable that advances in both could result in discoveries which could lead to an amicable synthesis.

Carl Sandburg relates a dialogue between a white American and Native American:

> The white man drew a small circle in the sand and told the red man, "This is what the Indian knows," and drawing a big circle around the small one, "this is what the white man knows." The Indian then took the stick and swept an immense ring around both circles and said, "this is where the white man and the red man know nothing." (1978)

In science, our focus on increasing the size of our circle of knowledge, and success in doing so, may have blinded us to the vast area of knowledge still uncreated. But in this story, even the Native American sees knowledge as a fixed and finite objective reality. But knowledge and reality are not fixed at all; they are created by acts of human imagination and as such are always destined to create new frontiers. In other words, there is no outer circle, no boundary. Knowledge will grow forever, with new knowledge creating fresh opportunities for creating yet more knowledge. There will be no end. There is no chance of religious beliefs ever being squeezed out of existence, so to speak, and hence religious believers need not feel that their world is being shrunk by a hostile, invading scientific army.

It is interesting to see how this alternative view of scientific knowledge might impinge on the long-running controversy between evolution and creationism. We have already observed that despite the earnest efforts of the scientific and education community to teach evolution by natural selection, beliefs about creation that lie outside this naturalist framework seem to be remarkably resilient and robust. For some scientists, this state of affairs causes some amazement and despair because they fear that they are somehow failing in their educational mission.

The situation is actually worse than simply not believing that life on this planet evolved according to Darwin's model. Even apart from the widespread belief in mainstream religious dogmas, surveys regularly indicate that large numbers of people also believe in astrology, UFOs, superstitions, witchcraft, psychic phenomena, and many other things for which the scientific community has found no evidence and which are frowned on even by organized religions. Few daily newspapers are without a horoscope section, and one can see advertisements everywhere for fortune tellers who use various flamboyant techniques to predict the future.

Scientists argue that fairly simple tests will show that many of these superstitious beliefs are false and that fortune tellers, faith healers, and other claimants to supernatural powers are charlatans who are manipulating a gullible public for private gain. Those who worry about this phenomenon are perplexed as to why people are so perverse as to ignore the overwhelming evidence that science has amassed over the years. The temptation is to blame this state of affairs on popular culture and the education system, particularly teachers. If science were taught and understood by the students properly, the argument runs, then students would be able to see these superstitious beliefs are false. Hence there are frequent calls for better training of science teachers and for requiring students to take more science courses.

But part of the problem is our current view of what constitutes scientific knowledge, and this view colors how science is taught. Science is taught as if a few exceptionally gifted people have built a vast storehouse of knowledge that explains how the world works. Students are given the impression that they can learn some small portion of this knowledge, but the rest of the knowledge they will have to accept on faith.

This is not all that different from religion. Instead of religious leaders claiming to reveal the truth, it is scientists who claim to understand how the world works. Thus students are given two sets of received truths from which they must choose. Students are not in a position to evaluate the merits of either set because they have little experience in deciding for themselves how to choose between two theoretical structures. There always has been some authority figure telling students which theory is correct and should be believed. When, as adults, these students must choose between two theoretical structures, it becomes a matter of personal preference. It should not be surprising if they opt for belief structures that seem to have more relevance to their daily lives and that appear to add greater value and hope to their existence, even if it appears hopelessly irrational to scientists.

Another part of the problem is that there is something fundamentally flawed about trying to apply the scientific method to all beliefs. Scientific truths always have been, even in the traditional sense, only provisionally true. And creationists have realized that it is extremely difficult to determine what is absolutely true and

SCIENCE AND RELIGION: A POSSIBLE SOLUTION

what is false. If that is the case, creationists argue, why should people be forced to believe in scientific explanations over religious ones?

The position taken in this book, that scientific progress is not necessarily leading us toward the truth, may seem like another, and perhaps fatal, blow against science, destroying its already weakened authority in the struggle against superstition. I do not believe this is the case. If we can convince people that *all* knowledge is valid but that the goal of scientific knowledge is to achieve greater control over the environment (as opposed to greater "truth") and that it does this by constructing paradigms and refining and even overthrowing them as needed, then there will be a clear distinction between the knowledge created by science and that created by religion. In that way, scientific beliefs can be contrasted with religious beliefs more clearly than they are now.

Scientists are always seeking to extend the boundaries of their paradigms by exploring those areas that are not understood. They are not averse to seeking out situations that hold the promise of overthrowing the current paradigm. There is no set of core beliefs that is inherently immune from this scrutiny, though the practice of successful normal science requires that the scientific community tenaciously protect cherished theories from overthrow.

Religious belief structures, by contrast, usually have an unchanging core; and followers do not seek to extend their boundaries by seeking out situations where the existing religious belief structure is weakest and most likely to fail. They do not probe for inconsistencies or periodically replace their old beliefs with new ones in the light of new knowledge. Indeed, the unchanging nature of core religious beliefs is considered to be one of its main virtues, a reflection of its eternal truth.

Anomalies, which are key elements in the process of scientific progress, are not welcome in the religious context. Paradigm elucidation, refinement, and overthrow, which is the essence of the scientific enterprise, would be seen as a serious weakness for religion. So scientific and religious knowledge are created by different mechanisms and thus represent different kinds of knowledge. Since knowledge creates reality, they must represent different realities.

Of course, not everyone will, or even should, be persuaded to accept the scientific worldview for all situations. People believe things for a wide range of reasons, and religious beliefs satisfy a need that science cannot fill. People who have such a need will believe in religion regardless of what science may say. But if scientists say that scientific knowledge is true or approaching truth, then they are asserting something that cannot be justified. It is just another dogmatic assertion. Such an approach merely ends up forcing people to choose between what they perceive to be two contrasting dogmas; and if they want to be internally consistent in their beliefs, they must adopt one dogma and reject the other (Singham 2000b). This is the basic cause of the conflict between naturalism and creationism. But there is no compelling reason to force people into making such a drastic choice.

Science education in schools should be aimed at making students aware of the mechanism of paradigm creation, elucidation, refinement, crisis, and overthrow. It is easy to demonstrate how this process has resulted in theories that have increased our control over the environment, and the goal of scientific knowledge is greater control and predictability over our environment. This particular process of knowledge creation is what defines science and properly determines what belongs in a science curriculum.

Religious beliefs do not represent the same kind of knowledge as science because religious knowledge is not created in the same way as it is in science. Thus religious beliefs do not belong in schools as part of science education. But this does not mean that religious beliefs should be kept out at all costs. Most students have some sort of religious beliefs, and these views should be treated respectfully.

The debate between science and religion is influenced strongly by the issue of whether an objective reality exists. Quantum mechanics, one of the best theories we have in physics, argues against an objective reality. This absence of an objective reality allows for the possibility that the different ways in which science and religion create knowledge (the former by paradigm creation and overthrow, the latter by revelation) are leading to different, non-overlapping areas of knowledge. They need not be in fundamental contradiction.

It is a mistake to look for some carefully crafted formula that can be used to demarcate the line between science and religion and then to invoke the U.S. Constitution to banish religious beliefs from the classroom. This was the strategy adopted by the anti-creationist forces that successfully argued for striking down the Arkansas and Louisiana "balanced treatment" statutes. Such lines cannot be drawn in an intellectually honest way, and they end as mere legal strategies that do a disservice to both science and the philosophy of science.

Instead, any set of beliefs held by students that influence their thinking about the world can and should belong in the science classroom. However, those beliefs that are included should be subjected to examination according to the rules of paradigm development.

Much of the debate between the creationist and naturalist camps is irrelevant. However, once freed from belief in an objective reality and the value judgments that the term *truth* implies, with all the resulting passions that it arouses, the debate between science and religion can take place in its appropriate context. This would consist of addressing such questions as: What is the purpose of any particular form of knowledge? How does that knowledge develop and accumulate? What conditions aid its growth? How do we judge the usefulness of its result? What value does it add to the human condition? In such a discussion, there is room for scientific and religious knowledge to coexist meaningfully. People then can make informed judgments about which knowledge is useful to them in which context. They will become more discriminating judges of knowledge and thus better equipped to handle an increasingly complex, information-rich future.

CHAPTER TEN

SCIENCE AND TRUTH

> Physical concepts are free creations of the human mind,
> and are not, however it may seem, uniquely determined by
> the external world.
>
> — Albert Einstein

Scientists rarely discuss the philosophy of science. It is not that scientists do not consider themselves philosophers; they do, and they take great pride in being philosophers. However, most practicing scientists feel that philosophy arises naturally out of scientific activity and does not need any separate, formal study. Their philosophical outlook is picked up incidentally in the course of their training as scientists, by "doing science," rather than by reading about it. In addition, scientists pride themselves on working on problems that, however esoteric, promise to have definite answers, and they suspect that the issues addressed by philosophers of science are either trivially obvious or purely semantic and can never be resolved. Formal philosophy is something that is tangential to scientists' concerns.

Recently the scientific community has been beleaguered. After a period of spectacular growth fueled by the Cold War and space race, public support for science leveled off. The cancellation of the particle physics accelerator called the Superconducting Supercollider symbolized the end of the deferential attitude that policy makers had toward requests for support from the scientific community. These policy makers now ask much more critical questions about why this kind of knowledge should be pursued. The conventional answer — "Because it is there, it enriches our

culture, and will provide unimaginable technological spin-offs"
— is no longer sufficient. Policy makers now look for a more
immediate and practical return on the investment.

At the same time, scientists perceive rising public discontent
with science and a growing irrationalism. As one physicist argued
in an electronic newsletter:

> The embrace of irrationalism in academic disciplines
> ranging from literature and history to anthropology has been
> explored for the past three days at a conference sponsored
> by the New York Academy of Sciences. The postmodern
> view is that there is no such thing as objective truth: Science
> is a product of the power structure it serves, and scientific
> "laws" would come out differently in a different culture. A
> platoon of distinguished academics lamented the spread of
> this corrosive notion and recounted examples of the foolish-
> ness it engenders, but there were few proposals for how to
> deal with the problem. How can you debate someone who
> denies the existence of objective reality? In contrast to the
> gray-haired speakers, there was a significant representation
> of under-thirty social scientists in the audience. It seemed
> clear that not one of them believed a single word of what
> was being said. (Park 1995)

Many reasons have been put forward to explain the seeming
rise in irrational beliefs and the corresponding decline in the prestige of science. One group that is blamed is the philosophers of
science. Indeed, a particularly interesting and illuminating controversy erupted in the journal, *Nature*, in 1987. Two physicists,
T. Theocharis and M. Psimopoulos of Imperial College, London,
began with a scathing attack on the eminent philosophers of science
Karl Popper, Imre Lakatos, Thomas Kuhn, and Paul Feyerabend,
all of whose views have been discussed in previous chapters of
this book. The physicists argued that the epistemology of science
expounded by these four philosophers was indirectly destroying
public support for scientific research.

Theocharis and Psimopoulos had three main theses:

1. The four philosophers of science have sought to promote the false idea that the pursuit of scientific knowledge has no relation to the quest for objective truth.
2. This has undermined the prestige of science in the public eye and has caused a loss of support for scientific activities.
3. Scientists themselves are largely to blame for this sorry state of affairs because they actually admire the work of these philosophers and do not realize that, by quoting them approvingly, scientists are destroying themselves.

The article ends with a rallying cry for all scientists to realize the danger they are in and to unite in refuting the false and destructive ideas of these philosophers of science. Thus scientists would bring about a return to the age when science and scientists were much admired as impassioned and impartial searchers of truth and when support for scientific research was generous.

Critics were quick to point out that Theocharis and Psimopoulos present no evidence whatsoever that the politicians and administrators who ultimately decide on the levels of funding for science spend any time reading the latest philosophical journals before making their decisions on what kind of science to fund. Also, the assertion that scientists were to blame for approving of the philosophers probably surprised many scientists who may not have even heard of these philosophers, let alone approved of their views.

But the main substance of Theocharis and Psimopoulos' criticisms lies in their first point, and at first glance it does look as if there are irreconcilable differences between the conclusions of philosophers of science and of scientists themselves on the methods and goals of science. Scientists seem to believe that their pursuit of knowledge is bringing us closer to something that we call "the truth." Philosophers of science seem to be believe that there is nothing in the history of scientific progress or in its methods of development that gives support to that notion. It seems as if one or the other school of thought must be at least in partial error.

There are three common assumptions underlying the viewpoints of both the scientific community and the philosophers of science. These assumptions are the belief in the existence of an objective reality, scientific reductionism as a valid epistemology, and the idea that all knowledge (both realized and potential) sum up to a finite and unchanging amount. If the validity of these three assumptions is granted, then the conclusions of the two schools of thought are indeed incompatible and a conflict is inevitable. However, there is no reason to believe that *any* of those assumptions is true, and there is some reason to doubt it. If we are willing to give up these assumptions, then it is possible to arrive at a coherent worldview that brings together the scholarship in philosophy and in science.

Relinquishing the above three assumptions is not going to be easy for many to accept, especially within the scientific community, since they lie at the core of our belief structures. Ironically, the hardest thing to give up will be the idea of an objective reality. I say ironically because in Chapter 7 we saw that the acceptance of quantum mechanics as a complete theory (something which most physicists unquestioningly believe) necessarily implies the rejection of an objective reality (something that physicists are reluctant to accept). This was the key point of contention that Einstein was emphasizing even earlier than 1935. Yet physicists today tend to ignore this fact. It is as if they want to believe that quantum mechanics is a complete theory as well as to believe in an objective reality, though the two beliefs are fundamentally incompatible. The physicist quoted above was asking a rhetorical question when he wrote, "How can you debate someone who denies the existence of objective reality?" The physicist was sure that the physics community would overwhelmingly support his contention that people who reject objective reality are irrational and cannot be engaged in meaningful debate.

However, it is advances in physics that have provided the most persuasive arguments for the rejection of objective reality and it is physicists who should most welcome its demise. In the epic intellectual struggle between Einstein and his contemporaries over the question of whether an objective reality exists, Einstein was firmly on the side of the person in the street in his belief in an objective reality. But he was the one who lost the debate within the physics community. As is so often the case with great struggles, people tend to remember only the victors and vanquished and forget what the struggle was about. Many physicists now seem to remember only the winners and losers in that famous battle and have forgotten that Einstein's defeat automatically meant the rejection of an objective reality.

John Bell, the theoretical physicist whose remarkable theorem and the consequences it unleashed was discussed in Chapter 7, struggled to make sense out of what he had caused — the undermining of the belief in an objective reality and truth. He quotes others who say that it is not quantum mechanics that is peculiar, "rather the concepts of 'real' or 'complete truth' are generally mirages. The only legitimate notion of truth is 'what works.' And quantum mechanics certainly 'works'." But while agreeing that this position is intellectually consistent, Bell was not sure if this was the final word on the subject. He goes on to say: "However, the notion of 'real' truth, as distinct from a truth that is presently good enough for us, has also played a positive role in the history of science. . . . I can well imagine a future phase in which this happens again, in which the world becomes more intelligible to human beings, even to theoretical physicists, when they do not imagine themselves to be the centre of it" (Bell 1987).

A superficial reading of what I've written may give the impression that this book has been primarily a defense of the contributions of the philosophy of science and that I am another one of those "useful idiots" condemned by Theocharis and Psimopoulos, unwittingly aiding in the destruction of science. The rejection of an *objective* reality is commonly misinterpreted as a rejection of reality itself, and consequently a rejection of science. The rejection of reductionism also is frequently misunderstood as a criticism of physics in general and of particle physics in particular. It is not my intent to make either of those cases. Nothing useful ever comes of attempts by one academic discipline to establish an intrinsic superiority over another. Such debates usually are just an exercise in which holders of different worldviews and different premises talk *through* each other, reiterating what is best about their own fields and belittling the contributions of others.

What I have tried to do is to propose an alternative view of the scientific method and of where it leads. I cannot answer the question of whether the model is true; that type of question misses the point of the exercise. The best we can hope for in the development of knowledge is to seek explanations that are relatively free of internal contradictions, are consistent with the historical record, and provide a coherent worldview. What has been proposed here, like Darwin's theory of evolution by natural selection for biological change, does provide an explanation for knowledge growth that is consistent with historical events. What it also attempts to show is that philosophers of science have very important things to teach scientists and that, contrary to the views of Theocharis and Psimopoulos, a deep understanding of their views could lead us to a better understanding of our own scientific subdiscipline and its relationship to others. Scientists are pursuing truth, but the methods of science are not necessarily guaranteed to lead us to *the* truth or the *complete* truth.

It is unfortunate, as the philosophers of science pointed out, that our scientific destiny is not as grand or as expansive as scientists might like to believe; but, in itself, that is not sufficient grounds for rejecting the philosophers views, unless we wish to become mere propagandists for science. Part of the scientific folklore is that the "errors" of the past were caused largely by scientists extending their belief in the then current theories beyond the regions of their tested validity and then dogmatically clinging to them despite contrary evidence. T. H. Huxley's warning that "New truths of science begin as heresy, advance to orthodoxy, and end up as superstition" should encourage us to be open-minded about our understanding of scientific epistemology.

Although the criticisms raised by Theocharis and Psimopoulos against philosophers of science may have their origins in the mundane context of funding for scientific research, the issues raised by them have much broader implications. It is true that a knowledge of the epistemology of science is not necessary for a scientist to be good at his or her profession, as long as the goal of the profession is understood to be the development and refinement of paradigms within a subdiscipline and increasing control over the environment. However, as soon as one tries to embed this in a wider context, such as the search for "truth" or measuring the relative importance of disciplines, then one is forced to take seriously the analyses of those who have made a profound contribution to this subject. And however much one might dislike their conclusions, the work of Popper, Lakatos, Kuhn, and Feyerabend, as well as the works of Larry Laudan and David Bloor, stand out as landmarks in this field.

There is one important question that I have not addressed. That is whether there are *any* universal scientific truths that are independent of our choice of paradigms. In other words, if we were to encounter extraterrestrials whose scientific knowledge had evolved quite differently than did our own, would there be any conclusions at all that we would have in common? While it is plausible that more complex theories, such as quantum mechanics and relativity, could be human constructs that have no universal validity, there are other laws that are so simple and easy to understand that it is hard to see how they could not be universal. One such case is the law that states that the speed of light in a vacuum is the same for all observers irrespective of how they are moving. The concept of speed is so intuitive and its measurement so direct that it is hard to imagine an alternative framework. But while it is tempting to think that such a law must be universal, the lack of a viable alternative may be due simply to our lack of imagination.

These views may make many people uneasy because we have become accustomed to deferring to authority figures who tell us what is true and what we should believe. The general public is believed to lack the skills to make these judgments, especially when it comes to profound questions. While I have been careful to argue that we can retain the belief that science works, that it is worthwhile, rational, and progressing, without believing that it leads inexorably to the truth, there are many who will argue that this is too subtle a distinction for the general public. They will be apprehensive that most people will see this as an admission of weakness for science and will turn away from science even more.

I do not think this is the case. Although we pay lip-service to scientific literacy, what we usually mean by that phrase is getting the public to believe what the scientific community wants them to know and believe. Real literacy comes only when people understand what knowledge is, how it is created, what it represents, and how to judge its validity and usefulness. If we really want that, then we have to have confidence that people will understand the complexities of complex arguments. If we really want a high level of scientific literacy among members of the general public, then we have to shift our concerns from *what* people believe to making them conscious of *why* they believe what they do. That is when critical thinking will blossom.

This model of scientific knowledge is also not likely to lead to an end to science. Scientists have always, by and large, tended to ignore the philosophy of science as not very helpful to them in their work, and there is no reason to think that the situation is going to change. In general, the scientific community views *any* model of knowledge with skepticism. As Einstein said, the scientist "must appear to the systematic epistemologist as a type of unscrupulous opportunist: he appears as a *realist* in so far as he seeks to describe a world independent of the acts of perception; an *idealist* in so far as he looks upon the concepts and theories as the free inventions of the human spirit (not logically derivable from what is empirically given); a *positivist* in so far as he considers his concepts and theories justified only to the extent to which they furnish a logical representation of relations among sensory experiences. He may even appear as a *Platonist* or *Pythagorean* in so far as he considers the viewpoint of logical simplicity as an indispensable and effective tool of his research" (Pais 1982).

All journeys are presumed to have a destination. Sometimes we know what it is and look forward to it, at other times the end is hidden and we are apprehensive about what lies in store. The goal of the journey of knowledge, especially scientific knowledge, has always been presumed to be the revelation of the secrets of nature. Although we did not know what we would find at the end, or how much further we needed to go, or how long it would take us to get there, there usually was never any question that there *could* be an end, and the prospect of getting there has fuelled scientific curiosity for centuries. The burning desire to know has always been a characteristic of human development. It has been the engine that has driven scientific progress.

The tremendous success that science has had so far seemed to rest on two foundations. One was the belief in an objective reality, the other was the belief that the methods of science were bringing us closer to understanding that objective reality. But quantum mechanics seems to argue against the first belief, and philosophers of science have demonstrated that there is no evidence supporting the second belief.

So is the nature of scientific knowledge different in any way from that, say, of religion or musical knowledge? The answer is yes and no. Different kinds of knowledge are defined by the process by which they are created and not by anything intrinsic to each field. So scientific knowledge, with its method of paradigm creation and refinement, is different from those disciplines that follow different routes to knowledge creation. They just have different paradigms and different methods of new knowledge creation.

The method of paradigm refinement and overthrow that we find in science undoubtedly leads to greater control over the environment and thus to technological progress. Science works, and it works exceedingly well. Music does not need such control over the environment and thus has no need for the methods of science. Instead, music's process of knowledge accumulation allows the potential unleashing of the creative spirit in everyone. Science also could benefit from this opening of the creative door without losing the benefits that paradigm creating has brought. In *The Two Cultures*, C.P. Snow worried about the adverse consequences arising from the divergent paths that the sciences and humanities were taking. Perhaps this unleashed creativity in science could be the bridge that spans the two cultures, creating a new union of all knowledge that everyone can enjoy and from which everyone can benefit.

The model of scientific knowledge that has been presented in this book is at once both depressing and exhilarating, depending on one's point of view. Those scientists who have worked feverishly to unearth what they believe would be the *final* piece of the puzzle, the ultimate secrets of the universe, will find the model depressing because it implies that whatever progress we make, however spectacular our discoveries and advances, we will *never* know everything. Every new discovery we make, rather than reducing our ignorance by eliminating false theories and beliefs, actually opens up many new avenues of investigation. There is no final answer and never will be.

BIBLIOGRAPHY

Anderson, P.W. "Some Thoughtful Words (Not Mine) on Research Strategy for Theorists." *Physics Today* 43 (February 1990): 9.

Arons, Arnold B. *A Guide to Introductory Physics Teaching.* New York: John Wiley, 1990.

Aspect, A.; Dalibard, J.; and Roger, G. "Experimental Test of Bell's Inequality Using Time-Varying Analyzers." *Physical Review Letters* 49 (1982): 1804-1807.

Behe, Michael J. *Darwin's Black Box.* New York: Free Press, 1996.

Bell, John S. *Speakable and Unspeakable in Quantum Mechanics.* Cambridge: Cambridge University Press, 1987.

Berliner, David C., and Biddle, Bruce J. *The Manufactured Crisis: Myths, Fraud, and the Attack on America's Public Schools.* Reading, Mass.: Addison-Wesley, 1995.

Bernstein, Jeremy. *Quantum Profiles.* Princeton, N.J.: Princeton University Press, 1991.

Bloor, David. *Knowledge and Social Imagery.* London: Routledge and Kegan Paul, 1976.

Bracey, Gerald W. "The Second Bracey Report on the Condition of Public Education." *Phi Delta Kappan* 74 (October 1992): 104-17.

Brooks, Jacqueline Grennon, and Brooks, Martin G. *In Search of Understanding: The Case for Constructivist Classrooms.* Alexandria, Va.: Association for Supervision and Curriculum Development, 1993.

Dawkins, Richard. *Climbing Mount Improbable.* New York: W.W. Norton, 1996.

Einstein, A.; Podolsky, B.; and Rosen, N. "Can Quantum Mechanical Description of Physical Reality Be Considered Complete?" *Physical Review* 47 (15 May 1935): 777.

"Evolution and the Bible." *Ohio Academy of Science Newsletter* (Spring 1995): 5.

Faure, Gunter. *Principles of Isotope Geology.* New York: John Wiley & Sons, 1986.

Feyerabend, Paul K. *Against Method.* 3rd ed. London: Verso, 1993.

Feynman, R.P. *International Journal of Theoretical Physics* 21 (1982): 471.

Gish, Duane T. *Evolution? The Fossils Say No!* San Diego: Creation-Life, 1981.

Glanz, James. "Measurements Are the Only Reality, Say Quantum Tests." *Science* 270 (1 December 1995): 1439.

Godfrey, Laurie R., ed. *Scientists Confront Creationism*. New York: W.W. Norton, 1983.

Gould, Stephen Jay. "Impeaching a Self-Appointed Judge." *Scientific American* (July 1992): 118-21.

Gould, Stephen Jay. *Rocks of Ages : Science and Religion in the Fullness of Life*. New York: Ballantine, 1999.

Gross, Paul R., and Levitt, Norman. *Higher Superstition: The Academic Left and Its Quarrels with Science*. Baltimore: Johns Hopkins University Press, 1994.

Gross, Paul R.; Levitt, Norman; and Lewis, Martin W., eds. *The Flight from Science and Reason*. New York: New York Academy of Sciences, 1996.

Hardin, Garrett James. *Nature and Man's Fate*. New York, Rinehart, 1959.

Hively, William. "How Much Science Does the Public Understand?" *American Scientist* 76 (September-October 1988): 439-44.

Hoke, Franklin. "Scientists See Broad Attack Against Research and Reason." *The Scientist* 9 (10 July 1995).

Horgan, John. *The End of Science: Facing the Limits of Knowledge in the Twilight of the Scientific Age*. New York: Addison-Wesley, Helix, 1996.

Huxley, Thomas Henry. *Darwiniana*. New York: D. Appleton and Company, 1896.

Johnson, Phillip E. *Darwin on Trial*. Washington, D.C: Regnery Gateway, 1991.

Kolb, David A. *Experiential Learning*. New Jersey: Prentice-Hall, 1984.

Kuhn, Thomas S. *The Structure of Scientific Revolutions*. 2nd ed. Chicago: University of Chicago Press, 1970.

Lakatos, Imre. T*he Methodology of Scientific Research Programmes*. New York: Cambridge University Press, 1978.

Larson, Edward J., and Witham, Larry. "Scientists Are Still Keeping the Faith." *Nature* 386 (April 1997): 435-36.

Larson, Edward J., and Witham, Larry. "Scientists and Religion in America." *Scientific American* (September 1999): 88-93.

Laudan, Larry. *Science and Relativism: Some Key Controversies in the Philosophy of Science*. Chicago: University of Chicago Press, 1990.

Laudan, Larry. *Beyond Positivism and Relativism: Theory, Method, and Evidence*. Boulder, Colo.: Westview, 1996.

Lederman, Leon M., and Teresi, Dick. *The God Particle: If the Universe Is the Answer, What Is the Question?* Boston: Houghton Mifflin, 1993.

Mermin, N.D. "Is the Moon There When Nobody Looks? Reality and Quantum Theory." *Physics Today* 38, no. 4 (1985): 38.

National Academy of Sciences Committee on Science and Creationism. *Science and Creationism: A View from the National Academy of Sciences*. Washington, D.C.: National Academy Press, 1984.

Numbers, Ronald L. *The Creationists: The Evolution of Scientific Creationism*. New York: Alfred A. Knopf, 1992.

Pais, Abraham. *"Subtle Is the Lord": The Science and Life of Albert Einstein*. Oxford: Oxford University Press, 1982.

Park, Robert. "What Can Be Done About the Flight from Science and Reason?" *What's New*. Electronic newsletter of the American Physical Society. 2 June 1995. http://www.aps.org/WN/WN95/wn060295.html.

Park, Robert. "Book Review: Intelligent Designer Meets the Blind Watchmaker." *What's New*. Electronic newsletter of the American Physical Society. 27 December 1996. http://www.aps.org/WN/WN96/wnl22796.html.

Popper, Karl R. *Conjectures and Refutations: The Growth of Scientific Knowledge*. New York: Basic Books, 1962.

Ruse, Michael. *But Is It Science?* Buffalo, N.Y.: Prometheus, 1988.

Sandburg, Carl. *Breathing Tokens*. New York: Harcourt Brace Jovanovich, 1978.

Simpson, George Gaylord. *Tempo and Mode in Evolution*. New York: Columbia University Press, 1944.

Singham, Mano. "The Science and Religion Wars." *Phi Delta Kappan* 81 (February 2000): 424-32.a

Singham, Mano. "Teaching and Propaganda." *Physics Today* 53 (June 2000): 54-55.b

Snow, C.P. *The Two Cultures: And a Second Look*. 2nd. ed. Cambridge: University Press, 1964.

Tagliabue, John. "Pope Bolsters Church's Support for Scientific View of Evolution." *New York Times*, 25 October 1996.

Theocharis, T., and Psimopoulos, M. "Where Science Has Gone Wrong." *Nature* 329 (15 October 1987): 595-98.

Tuana, Nancy, ed. *Feminism & Science*. Bloomington: Indiana University Press, 1989.

Weinberg, Steven. "Newtonianism, Reductionism, and the Art of Congressional Testimony." *Nature* 330 (3 December 1987): 433-37.

Weinberg, Steven. *Dreams of a Final Theory*. New York: Vintage, 1994.

Whitcomb, John C., Jr., and Morris, Henry M. *The Genesis Flood*. Philadelphia: Presbyterian and Reformed Publishing Company, 1961.

Whitehead, Alfred North. *The Aims of Education and Other Essays*. New York: Macmillan, 1929.

Zeilik, Michael, and Gaustad, John. *Astronomy: The Cosmic Perspective*. New York: Harper & Row, 1983.

ABOUT THE AUTHOR

Mano Singham was born in Sri Lanka and obtained his B.Sc. in physics from the University of Colombo in Sri Lanka. His master's and doctoral degrees in theoretical nuclear physics are from the University of Pittsburgh.

Singham has taught and carried out research at the University of Rochester, Los Alamos National Laboratory, Drexel University, the University of Pittsburgh, and the University of Colombo. Since 1989 Singham has been on the faculty at Case Western Reserve University, where he teaches in the Physics Department and also serves as Associate Director of the University Center for Innovations in Teaching and Education.

Photograph by Shermila Singham.

MANO SINGHAM
30-MINUTE VIDEOTAPE

Mano Singham discusses his work on "The Science/Religion Debate" in this 30-minute videotape, which is part of Phi Delta Kappa's **Further Thoughts** series. This series features authors whose articles have appeared in the *Phi Delta Kappan.* Singham's article, "The Science and Religion Wars," was featured in the February 2000 issue of the *Kappan.*

Phillip Harris, former director of PDK's Center for Professional Development and Services, who created the video series, commented, "Our objective was to go beyond the article." Singham's discussion of the issues involved in the science/religion debate offers insights that will inform education policy and practice.

30-minute videotape
$29.95 (PDK members, $19.95) + s&h

ORDER BY PHONE: 1-800-766-1156
Major credit cards accepted.

Or send an institutional purchase order to Phi Delta Kappa International, P.O. Box 789, Bloomington, IN 47402-0789. Include $5 shipping and handling charge for each video. Indiana residents add 5% sales tax. Purchase orders and credit card orders also are accepted by fax at (812) 339-0018.